Steward
Living as Disciples in Everyday Life

Participant's Manual

General Editors

Bruce C. Birch
Charles R. Foster

Abingdon Press
Nashville

STEWARD
LIVING AS DISCIPLES IN EVERYDAY LIFE
Participant's Manual

Copyright © 2000 by Abingdon Press

ISBN, 068709934x

00 01 02 03 04 05 06 07 08 09 – 10 9 8 7 6 5 4 3 2 1

MANUFACTURED IN THE UNITED STATES OF AMERICA

CONTENTS

INTRODUCTION

Why should a congregation take on the study of the biblical role of the steward? Few people today talk about themselves as stewards. When they do, they usually refer to themselves as being stewards of some kind of resources—money or the environment for example. When we use the term in the church we tend to limit our usage to the financial campaign for the church budget. In both instances the larger notion of stewardship embodied in the role and work of "good stewards" in the Bible has been diminished, if not lost from our consciousness.

To understand what it means to be a disciple of Jesus Christ requires, however, that we eventually come to terms with the biblical notion of stewardship and of the role of the steward in the life of faith. It has to do with the ways in which we live out or practice that faith.

Through the centuries our faith ancestors took the responsibility of being stewards of the relationship of God to the world and to the whole human community quite seriously. The biblical record persistently encourages the Israelites to care for the land and do justice. Paul urges the early church to remember that the gospel entrusted to him is also entrusted to them.

After the Reformation, some churches, especially the Methodists, called the elected leaders of their congregations Boards of Stewards. Their responsibilities included not only the upkeep or stewardship of church property, but also the maintenance of the spiritual and physical well-being of their members. Stewards in Caribbean Methodist churches, for example, continue this practice by taking money given by church members to the poor in their communities.

We invite you therefore to explore the possibilities to be found in reclaiming the calling to be "good stewards" in our own lives, that is, to explore ways to live in the world as contemporary disciples of Jesus Christ. We refer to these ways as "practices." Dorothy Bass and Craig Dykstra, in their book, *Practicing Our Faith: A Way of Life for a Searching People,* have

defined practices as "things Christian people do together over time in response to and in light of God's active presence for the life of the world . . . Honoring the body. Hospitality. Household economics. Saying yes and no. Keeping Sabbath. Testimony. Discernment. Shaping communities. Forgiveness. Healing. Dying well. Singing our lives . . . ordinary practices, the stuff of everyday life."[1]

As participants in this study you and the other members of the group will share the following expectations of each other:

- Attendance at all sessions. If it is necessary to miss a session your commitments related to being prepared for the study and for the care of the members of the group should be maintained.
- Weekly preparation for the session. This commitment involves reading the Scripture texts each day so that they become familiar, as well as reading the content in the Participant's Manual and taking notes on your thoughts and reactions to both sets of readings during the week.
- Daily prayer for the members of the group, for the issues and concerns raised by group members, for the congregation and community in which you live and minister, and for the world which is the setting and provides the resources for our stewardship.
- Commitment to try out practices of being a steward. Each session will include opportunities for you to make decisions about these practices.

Welcome to this study! We hope that it will be an enriching journey for you as you explore the role of the steward in the Bible and in Christian life and as you make decisions about what it means to be a disciple of Jesus Christ in your everyday activities.

1 Craig Dykstra and Dorothy C. Bass, "Times of Yearning, Practices of Faith," *Practicing Our Faith: A Way of Life for a Searching People,* ed. Dorothy C. Bass (San Francisco: Jossey-Bass, 1997), p. 5.

BECOMING STEWARDS:
Practices That Shape Our Lives

Steward: Living as Disciples in Everyday Life asks us to think about what it means to be a steward of God's great gifts to us and to all humanity. As stewards we are called to care for all that God has created and given to us. Our lives as stewards are shaped primarily by our ordinary everyday activities. When we ask what it means to be a steward, we are asking what our Christian faith has to do with our work, our personal relationships, how we spend our money, our political life, and the way we raise our children. Simple daily practices shape our lives—practices such as family prayer, recycling our newspapers, listening to someone who needs a friend, saying "I love you" to members of our household. All of these things make us who we are.

During these next few weeks we will think together about the practices that shape our lives—the ordinary stuff of our daily lives. Do they help us live as faithful stewards? Are they responsive to God's active presence? Are there some new practices that we would like to cultivate and some old ones that we would like to let go? We may find that we want to make some changes in the way that we spend our time and our money, the way that we treat the created order, and the way that we live in community with one another.

Becoming faithful stewards in a culture that is built on practices of consumption and stress and materialism will not be easy, and it will be most difficult if we try to do it alone. During this study you and the other members of your group will be able to give and receive support as you begin some new practices in your daily lives. As you read the material for each session, the questions in the margins of this book will help you think about the practices that shape your life. When you meet together as a group you can help one another make realistic decisions about what you want to do each week. You will discover that the support of the group can be indispensable when internal habits and external pressures make it difficult to change.

Here are some questions to ask yourself as you think about practices you might want to begin or others you might want to let go:

- How will this practice help me pay closer attention to God's presence in my life?
- How will this practice help me participate in God's activity in the world?
- How have Christians through time shaped this practice?
- Is this practice concrete and specific—can I really do it?
- How will this affect my closest relationships?
- How will this affect my larger community?
- Is this something that can only be done individually, or is it also something that I might want to institute in my congregation?
- What kind of support will I need to make this change?

As you go through the study in the coming weeks, the support of your group and others will become your most important resource. You will discover that small changes will make big differences in your daily lives. The experience of each person will enrich the entire group as you begin a lifelong adventure of faithful stewardship.

Stewards of the Gospel

Bruce C. Birch

Read   *Isaiah 52:7-10*
         Isaiah 55: 6-11
         2 Corinthians
         5:14-21

During the Babylonian exile, the Hebrew people found themselves living in a place that seemed strange and alien to them. Their understanding of God's presence had been so closely tied to their homeland that they had to think in new ways about how God might be present in this foreign territory. For many of us, the beginning of the twenty-first century seems alien as well and we find ourselves asking the same questions that the Hebrew people asked: "How can we sing the Lord's song in a strange land?" As we face the strange land of our own future, there is a note of fear in such a question—a fear that our singing might be overcome by our anxieties and uncertainties, our problems and crises.

The prophets of the exile understood that to sing the Lord's song in the crises of any age requires a rootedness in the **memory** of the faith community on the one hand and the courage of **vision** in confidence that the future is God's future on the other. To remember the biblical and historical traditions of what God has done in the experience of those who went before us, and to dare to dream dreams and see visions of the possibilities that God is opening up for us, frees us from the tyranny and paralysis of present crises.

This study explores the role of steward in the life of God's community as an important guiding image for living as disciples in our everyday lives. It is a role that is both deeply rooted in our biblical and historical traditions and richly filled with possibilities for understanding our ongoing life as the people of God. A steward is a person given the responsibility for the care, management, and utilization of something that belongs to another. Yet, it is a role that implies trust and partnership on the part of the owner toward the steward. For Christians to claim the role of steward is to be reminded that all that we are and all that we have comes into our care as the gift of God. To be a steward is to be entrusted through God's grace, a role that seems especially appropriate for the proclaiming of grace in the life of the church. The various arenas in which we exercise the role of steward are all interrelated and are to be understood as arenas where we receive, reflect, and proclaim the grace of God. To be a steward is to be called to a vocation of God's grace.

List all the words and phrases you associate with stewardship.

The apostle Paul said, "In everything give thanks." How might you do that for a whole day?

The premise of *Steward: Living as Disciples in Everyday Life* is that all of us are called by God to be stewards. This first session provides the framework for the whole study. As your group meets together during the coming weeks, you will study a variety of Old and New Testament texts that will help you understand what it means to live as a steward. Sometimes you will discover that what the Scripture says to you is in conflict with the demands of the culture in which we live. Together you and the others in your group will be asked to explore some daily practices that might help you to live as faithful disciples in the midst of that tension.

Name some ways we can make visible the good news of God's redeeming grace.

We are called to be stewards of the gospel. As the church, the most fundamental gift entrusted to our stewardship is the good news that God who created the world and grieves over its brokenness is at work to redeem the world and restore it to wholeness. God's redeeming work has found its central focus in the life, death, and resurrection of Jesus Christ and will be completed in the full restoration of God's reign over all the earth. The stewardship of the gospel is the prologue and presupposition of all of our other practices as God's stewards. What we do and who we become in our use of God's gifts is shaped by our response to the gift of God's redeeming love in Jesus Christ that we are invited to share.

In what ways might we all think differently about our care of creation if we viewed ourselves as stewards and not masters?

We are called to be stewards of God's creation. Our very being and all those resources that enable our lives come as the gifts of God's creation. Creation is relational in character. We experience the wholeness God intended in creation only when we are harmoniously related to God, to others, and to the earth itself with all of its plants and animals. As human beings we are created in the image of God, which means that we represent the Creator in our dominion over the earth. This makes us stewards of the earth and not its masters. Our well-being depends on the well-being of the whole of creation, and our stewardship of the earth's resources is foundational for our personal, social, and economic life. In a culture that often idolizes self-sufficiency and ownership, our biblical faith calls us to recognize our interdependence on the whole of creation and our stewardship of resources that belong to God as true owner.

We are called to be stewards of community, but we are members of a variety of communities. To live as communities committed to God's purposes in the world generates a characteristic pattern for the practices of stewards. As the people of God we are called to be stewards of our own *faith communities.*

The world God created for wholeness and life has become characterized by brokenness and death. God is at work to redeem the world and has also raised up a community as partners in this work: first, in the covenant community of Israel and then, in the church of Jesus Christ.

These communities are called into being in response to God's acts of saving grace in Exodus and Resurrection. As members of the body of Christ, we recognize that God's redeeming grace is the source of our new life and restored wholeness. In recognizing, receiving, and responding to that gift of grace we, as the community of God's people, become a community of stewards. In our gathered life we remember, celebrate, and proclaim God's grace. In our ritual and symbols we, as a community of stewards, acknowledge the One we serve and the redeeming tasks into which God has invited us. This gathered life focuses in doxology, word, and sacrament. Beyond our gathered life we seek to live as God's stewards in the world. As a community we hold our members accountable for this mission in covenant with God and with one another. This covenant as God's stewards creates an alternative community to the communities of the world and their self-serving goals.

In our personal relationships, the practice of stewards is characterized by love. In Scripture this love is understood in two ways. First is the love we see in the covenant between God and Israel. This love is committed in faithful covenant to the well-being of another. Second is the self-giving love that the early church called *agape*. Both of these understandings of love include the interplay of love and judgment. It is still an expression of love to demand accountability. This love is the mark of our stewardship of all relationships when they are understood as gifts of God's grace: family, friendship, marriage, parenting, hospitality, and corporate fellowship (*koinonia*). The willingness of Jesus to lay down his life for the sake of others models the full expression of such love.

In our economic relationships, the practice of stewards is

Identify ways your congregation acts as an "owner."

Identify ways your congregation acts as a "steward."

What would we do differently if we treated one another as gifts of God and not as useful commodities?

What factors have the greatest influence on your economic decisions?

characterized by equity in the distribution of the resources required to meet basic human needs and to provide for enjoyment of human life. In our biblical tradition the stewardship of economic resources is related to sufficiency rather than excess, corporate sharing rather than private ownership, and open access rather than hoarding. Jesus spoke more often on economic matters than any other subject in the gospels and stressed giving as a crucial mark of faithful discipleship. Our practice as a community of stewards, if it is marked by these biblical understandings, will provide both critique and alternative to the frequent emphasis in our time on acquisition, consumption, and accumulation.

What are some ways you might act as a steward in political life?

In our political relationships, justice characterizes the practice of stewards. In Scripture, justice recognizes the right of all to have these needs for wholeness and well-being supported by the community. Participation, shared power, and channels for redress of grievance are crucial to the practice of stewards in the political arena. As a community of stewards we have a special concern for those who are exploited, oppressed, or marginalized. In our practice we are called to be advocates for those who have been denied justice. Jesus modeled such justice in his own association with and advocacy for the outcasts and marginalized of his own time. Indeed, to know Christ is to know him in "the least of these."

What is our responsibility as a steward to those who come after us?

We are called to be stewards of hope. As a community of God's stewards, we trust that our lives and all of human history originate in God and will be consummated in God. Thus, all of time itself is a gift given into our care as stewards. We can never live in the present moment as an end in itself, whether in the despair of crisis or in the careless pursuit of self-gratification. The biblical understanding of sabbath observance stands as a reminder of the gift of our days that God has given into our care. Because we know a past with God (memory) and trust that the future is also God's (vision), the community of stewards can live every present moment filled with the possibilities of hope. Our time cannot then be squandered in despair or self-satisfaction but must be used in the service of God's hopeful purposes and our partnership with those purposes as faithful stewards.

Signs and Symbols of Stewardship

Throughout Scripture, faithful stewards are known by the way in which they live, both as individuals and as communities. In the Old and New Testaments we find clearly identifiable practices that we might call the signs and symbols of stewardship. They are the marks of those who seek to live as households of God and communities of resurrection, grounded in the gospel of Jesus Christ. These symbols of stewardship ask that we live in ways that are contrary to the prevailing culture. We will need help and support from one another if they are to become the marks of our lives and the life of our congregation.

Keeping Sabbath

The heart of sabbath-keeping, a principle embedded in the Ten Commandments, is pausing to rest and remember our dependency on God. God is the Creator, and we are the creatures. Because sabbath reminds us of that relationship, the traditional Jewish sabbath rules forbid doing anything that demonstrates our mastery over creation. If we do such things we just might forget who is the creature in this relationship. And so we are asked to stop and pay attention to God.

In the Old Testament, sabbath had two sources—creation and Exodus. From the creation story comes our understanding of sabbath rest and from the Exodus story comes our understanding of sabbath justice. This rest to which God calls us is not only for us, it is also for all of creation. Having experienced slavery in Egypt when the relentlessness of work prevented sabbath rest, the Hebrew people were to be sure that they never prevented that rest on the part of others. Even those who did not practice their faith—the strangers and aliens in their midst, the animals who worked their fields—all were to be given rest.

We are tempted to think about sabbath-keeping only in terms of our individual lives. To keep sabbath certainly means attending worship, resting from our need to control our own world, perhaps spending time with friends, writing letters, or taking a walk in the woods. This is part of what it means to remember that God is the Creator and we are the creatures. But the justice perspective on sabbath-keeping may not be as easy to define. Protecting rest for others is

What are some ways that we can pause to rest and remember our dependency on God?

difficult to do in a culture where retail businesses flourish on their Sunday revenues. No longer do we have a common day of rest and so our sabbath-keeping has become a private affair. We must think together about what it means in our time to keep sabbath for ourselves and protect it for others.

Practicing Hospitality

For those who enjoy entertaining friends, inviting them for food and fellowship, hospitality in its popular definition sounds like a welcome characteristic for stewards. But the biblical notion of hospitality goes far beyond entertaining friends. It is about welcoming strangers and aliens—not the ones we know, the comfortable ones, the ones who look and act like us. Saint Benedict said to his monks, "Let everyone be received as Christ." This kind of hospitality is not so easy.

To offer hospitality is to provide a place where strangers are welcome and where they are accepted as they are, not asked to become like us. As more and more of us are isolated in our homes and neighborhoods, it is difficult to find ways to welcome strangers. Some congregations have begun providing warm places to sleep for homeless individuals during the winter. Preparing and serving dinner, spending the evening talking, staying overnight, and then providing breakfast can be wonderful ways of entertaining "angels unaware," as the writer of Hebrews says.

Congregations, households, and individuals who find ways to provide hospitality to the strangers and aliens in their midst discover another truth about God's hospitality: often the guest becomes the host and we become not only the bearer but also the recipient of gifts. As stewards of all God's gifts, we must ask who the strangers and aliens are in our lives and how we can welcome them in ways that free them to be themselves and enable us to receive their gifts.

Tithing

At least once a year most congregations are reminded that tithing is a biblical practice. When we are trying to raise money for the annual budget of the church, the verses from the Old Testament about giving 10 percent are recited in

What are some ways that we can offer hospitality to strangers and aliens in our midst?

many places. But it is important to hear not only the practice but also the question behind the practice: to whom does our money belong? Not just the percentage that we are giving to the church but all the rest as well.

The primary reason for the tithe in the Old Testament is to give to the poor. Unfortunately, in our consumer culture the word "tithe" conjures up images of legalism, compulsion, and fund-raising to support the programs and ministries of the church. It is not aimed at providing for the poor, nor do we very often view it as a joyous spiritual exercise that has more to do with celebration than budgets. In fact, if a congregation decided to be faithful to the practice of tithing, it might call on its members to give 10 percent of their income to the poor before they give to the church.

For those of us who want to live as faithful stewards of God's gifts, tithing is not a legalistic rule about how much we give but a beginning guideline that helps us decide how to care for the gift of money that we have received. In the New Testament, the tithe is not mentioned, but we see again and again examples of those who gave far beyond that measure in order to follow Jesus.

The questions faithful stewards ask are: To whom does our money belong? How does our spending reflect the deepest commitments of our hearts? Those of us who long to heal human hurts, nurture human souls, and relieve poverty and suffering must ask ourselves whether our expenditures tell the story of our commitments.

How does your spending reflect your deepest commitments?

Jubilee

The Old Testament includes not only the keeping of a weekly sabbath but also the keeping of a sabbath year every seventh year and a Jubilee year every fiftieth year, after seven sabbath years. The Jubilee year involved freeing the slaves, canceling debts, letting the land lie fallow, and returning the land to the original landowners. All of these provisions may not have been carried out, but Jubilee is a well-remembered principle that helps us know what God desires.

Through his ministry, Jesus called people to a new way of giving their whole lives to God. He talked more about money than almost any other subject and always reminded his followers that all we have belongs to God. He called them always to care for the weaker members of the society and

What are some ways we could carry out the Jubilee principle today?

his way of living leads us to ask not "How much of mine do I have to give up?" but "How much of God's do I keep?"

For those of us who want to live as stewards, we must wrestle with the ways that we can respond to the needs of our world today and tomorrow. The biblical practices may come to us from a far distant time and place and they may not seem to fit with our particular household. But at the very least they call us to be intentional about the way that we live in the world. They offer us some particular ways of ordering our lives. They call us to be faithful to a tradition that reminds us that our homes and our time and our resources do not belong to us. We are stewards of what belongs to God. Whether we are artists or engineers, homemakers or physicians, scientists or theologians, accountants or executives, government workers or church bureaucrats, all of us who love God and the world that God made are called to be a transforming presence in that world, stewards in the household of God.

Conclusion

As you meet together, we invite you to listen carefully to the word that the Scriptures speak to your own life and to explore in new ways what that would mean in your everyday activities. We hope that the group in which you participate will not only provide a place where you can test ideas and understandings as you study, but also a place where you will find support for exploring some new ways of living. To become a steward of the good news of Jesus Christ and live as his disciples has implications for all that you do. We hope that these weeks of study and fellowship will lead to deeper and more meaningful understandings of Scripture and God's call in your life and to new and enriching life practices.

Stewards of the Good News of Creation I

Mary Elizabeth Mullino Moore

Read *Genesis 1:26-31*
       Luke 12:42-48

Last week we talked about what it means to be stewards of all God's gifts. We are, first of all, to be stewards of the gospel, the good news of Jesus Christ that has been entrusted to our care. During the next few weeks we will talk about some of the specific ways that we are called to be stewards. We begin at the same place the Bible begins—creation. God has given us dominion over creation but too often we have believed that meant domination. We have seen creation as something to be used rather than to be cared for. This week and next we will be looking together for some new ways that we can be good stewards of the great gift of God's creation.

• • •

Then God said, "Let us make humankind in our image, according to our likeness; and let them have dominion over the fish of the sea, and over the birds of the air, and over the cattle, and over all the wild animals of the earth, and over every creeping thing that creeps upon the earth."

(Genesis 1:26)

This verse has perplexed and delighted readers of Genesis since the beginning of recorded biblical times. What does it mean to be created in the image of God? Why does God say "let *us*" and "according to *our* likeness"? Why does the text use a strong word like "dominion" in naming human responsibilities in God's creation?

These questions have long stirred Jewish and Christian people to wonder. Several years ago, when a group of church folk raised the question about dominion, a young Japanese woman, reading from her Japanese Bible, said, "Look! The Japanese translation says that human beings are to 'care for' the fish and birds and cattle." She explained that, while the Japanese language has other words for "rule," the word chosen

Make a list of the good things about creation.

to translate the ancient Hebrew is "care." In this interchange, we see the challenge for translators and faithful people who wonder about this Scripture passage. Naturally, we ask what it says to us as we seek to be stewards of God's good creation. In a questioning spirit, then, we enter the themes of this session—creation, community, and responsibility.

Stewards in Biblical Times

The two biblical texts for this session are rich in images of God and God's relationship with us, particularly as regards stewardship. The texts are also perplexing, and even more perplexing when we consider them together. Here is where our adventure begins, diving first into the wonders and mysteries of Genesis 1:24-31—a dramatic telling of the sixth day of creation.

In the Genesis text, we see God in many roles—Creator, Provider, Holy Community, Power-Sharer, Delegator, and Celebrant. Consider, first, God as **Creator**, the most obvious of God's roles in the first chapters of Genesis. We see the words repeated in rhythmic circles: "God made. . . ," "God created humankind," and "God saw everything that he had made."

Read the newspaper today and look for an example of injustice done to creation. How could you help right the injustice?

God's creative work overflows, but God is also **Provider**. In verse 26, God provides humans to have dominion (stewardship) over the animals. We might be tempted to see this as dominance by humans but, in the same verse, we are told that God will make people in God's own image—as stewards who will carry on God's work. But God not only provides humans for the animals; God also provides plants and trees for the people and animals to eat (Genesis 1:29-30). In a circle of interconnection, humans will care for animals, and plants will care for people and other animals by providing food.

The next three attributes of God are interrelated. One way to describe God is to say that God is **Holy Community**. God says, "Let *us* make humankind in *our* image." God's own multifaceted self created "humankind" (translated from the Hebrew *adam* meaning human rather than man) in God's image—"male and female he created them" (1:27). The image of God as plural, and as both male and female (or beyond gender), has caused much confusion, especially with the strong emphasis in Judaism and Christianity on

monotheism. There are images in other biblical texts in which God communicated through angels and other heavenly beings. Consider the angel of the Lord who appeared to Hagar (Genesis 16:7-13); the heavenly beings who appeared to Abraham and Sarah (18:1-15); the angels who appeared to Jacob on a ladder (28:12-13); the strange man who wrestled with Jacob until dawn (32:24-30); and the angel who appeared to Mary, announcing the birth of her son (Luke 1:26-38). The Christian doctrine of Trinity—one God in three Persons—helps us understand this multi-faceted God. The Holy Spirit, like a dove, descended from heaven at Jesus' baptism (Matthew 3:13-17; Mark 1:9-11; Luke 3:21-22). The Scriptures give us this very interesting and visionary image of God as Holy Community in which decisions are made communally ("Let us make humankind" in Genesis 1:26).

Closely related to the role of God as Holy Community are roles of God as **Power-Sharer** and **Delegator**. God shares creative power and delegates responsibility to the earth and nonhuman creation: "And God said, 'Let the earth bring forth living creatures of every kind'" (1: 24a; cf. 1:11). In a more indirect way, God delegates responsibility to plants to feed human beings and other animals. Certainly, God shares power with human beings and delegates them to be responsible for the rest of creation: "God said to them, 'Be fruitful and multiply, and fill the earth and subdue it; and have dominion . . .'" (1:28; cf. 1:26). According to the first chapter of Genesis, God is the Supreme Creator, but God invokes the help of human beings and the rest of creation. The circles of creation, and the ongoing circles of life, require all creatures to exercise God-given power and accept God-delegated responsibility.

This leads finally to one other role of God as **Celebrant**. The awesome responsibility of what has been said thus far is made possible because creation is good; God is the one who declares it so. What begins as a command on the sixth day of creation (as on other creation days of Genesis 1) ends with celebration. God is the Celebrant, who delights in creation and declares it *very good*!

Turning more briefly to the New Testament text, Luke 12:41-48, we see potent images of God, addressed to Luke's community as they await the return of Jesus. We find Peter asking Jesus if he is talking to the disciples or to everyone in telling the watchfulness parables (Luke 12:35-40). Typical of

List ways you practice stewardship of creation. Note which have the most potential for personal change.

Jesus, he does not answer the question directly; instead, he offers a collection of sayings about a "faithful and prudent manager," a hardworking slave (or servant, *doulos*), and slaves who are irresponsible. We see here a picture of God who gives responsibility (as in the Genesis text) and who acts as **Master** and **Judge**. The responsibilities given by the master are great—to manage the master's slaves and distribute their food. The responsibilities grow even larger for servants who do their work well; they are put in charge of all the master's possessions. Whether people are managers or servants, they are expected to carry on the master's work. The judgments are also great, however. We are told about how irresponsible and violent a slave might become in waiting for the master who is delayed. We hear how the master will come unexpectedly and cut that slave into pieces or cut him off. We hear that the punishment will be even greater for the slave who knew what his master wanted. The conclusion is ominous: "From everyone to whom much has been given, much will be required; and from the one to whom much has been entrusted, even more will be demanded" (12:48*b*). The text begins and ends with the note of responsibility, with the strong words of judgment in between.

Stewards in History

The diverse pictures of God in Genesis and Luke appear in many other biblical texts and church affirmations through history. The images intertwine as well. The Genesis idea of God as Power-Sharer and Delegator fits with Luke's emphasis on God as Master and Judge, giving abundant responsibility to people. Some images of God are more emphasized than others in Christian history, or they are presented in isolation from the complex picture of God's many images and roles. For example, God as Creator and Provider is accented more than God as Holy Community and Celebrant. When we attend to some images without others, or when Luke's sayings of Jesus are extracted from the rest of Luke or the rest of the Bible, a distorted picture of God emerges. Herein lies a challenge.

When the image of God as **Creator** has been separated from **Provider**, as during the Enlightenment of eighteenth-century Europe, God is identified as one who set creation in motion many centuries ago and was thereafter unavailable

to tend creation. This is the Unmoved Mover, or the Creator who leaves creation to take care of itself. In such a view, God is like an absentee landlord or a watchmaker, whose watches, once made, tick on without further guidance from the maker. Leaders of the Enlightenment often took such a view. They consequently placed high value on their own intellect and passed judgment on people different from themselves. Not unexpectedly, this Enlightenment mentality coexisted with extensive abuse of land and natural habitats, especially by powerful people and nations. It also coexisted with an extensive slave trade in European countries and the United States. Such mentality, however, is not consistent with the Genesis story of God, who created a world of stunning diversity and continually provides for it—for the light and dark, sea and dry land, plants and animals, human beings. God provides, in part, by creating an interwoven creation in which every part has a role to play for the sake of other parts.

List some ways this Enlightenment perspective has affected God's creation in your community.

A counterpoint to emerging Enlightenment ideas was sounded in eighteenth-century England by John Wesley and others. They argued that the stolen, enslaved people of Africa had souls; indeed, they were created in the image of God. And during the same century in England, many women argued that they also had souls and should, thus, be treated with the same respect and opportunities as men enjoyed. We see in both cases that people remembered and drew upon the biblical picture of human beings as created in the image of God. In both cases, many responsible Christians felt called to take responsibility by speaking out for others.

What are some environmental problems that might arise because of our lifestyles?

Other aspects of God's roles come into the foreground when we turn to other people and periods of history. Julian of Norwich was an English mystic who lived as a hermit between the thirteenth and fourteenth centuries. She dwelt strongly on the **Holy Community** and **Celebrant** roles of God, although she did not speak in those terms. She spoke repeatedly in Trinitarian language of God, and she saw the whole of God—Creator, Redeemer, Sustainer (also Father, Son, Spirit, and Father, Mother, Lover)—in a vision of something as small as a hazelnut. Drawing from her religious visions, Julian was able to celebrate the Trinitarian God who abides in and celebrates the smallest parts of God's vast creation.

When we think about God as **Power-Sharer** and **Delegator**, we find some hopeful stories in the high Middle

What changes might we make in our daily lives that would improve life a hundred years from now?

Name some of the things you are doing as you:

Create:

Provide:

Ages. In 1237, Archbishop Eberhard of Salzburg forbade the use of cleared forestlands so that the forests could grow again. Saint Francis of Assisi in twelfth- and thirteenth-century Italy spoke to birds and called for his monks to join him in simple living. These were people whose stories show that they understood that God had delegated responsibility to them and had given them the power to exercise that responsibility. From the standpoint of Luke's story of Jesus, these were people who, as manager (the Archbishop) and servant (Saint Francis), took the responsibility and power they were given. They recognized, in their distinctive ways, that God was **Master** and **Judge**, and they lived with a sense of obligation to care for God's creation.

Stewards in Our Time

If Genesis 1 reveals God as Creator, Provider, Holy Community, Power-Sharer, Delegator, and Celebrant, what does the same Scripture reveal about us as human beings? Most simply, if human beings are created in God's image, we too are creators, providers, holy community, power-sharers, delegators, and celebrants. Our body-mind-spirit is created in the divine image, and we are created to be in community with God and creation. This view sharply contrasts with contemporary views that deny or belittle the body. It does not allow us to see ourselves as autonomous individuals who care only about our own interests or the interests of our immediate family, friends, and associates.

The language of God's image can feed the arrogance of human beings, but human-centeredness is not compatible with the creation story in Genesis 1:1–2:4a. The world is already created quite well before the sixth day when human beings finally appear. Although some people argue that humans are the apex of creation, one can also argue that humans are the most dependent of all God's creatures. Further, God speaks them into existence with two breaths—one to name them as created in God's image and the other to give them responsibility (dominion) over the rest of creation. We are not created to be arrogant but to be responsible stewards. We are expected to **create** ("be fruitful and multiply" in Genesis 1:28a); we are expected to **provide** for other parts of creation ("have dominion" in 1:28b). We are expected to **live in holy community**, sharing the earth with other creatures of God and eating the fruits

of the earth (a vegetarian perspective on food in this particular creation account). We are further expected to **share power** with the earth, which is called to "bring forth living creatures" (1:24). We are even expected to **delegate** or honor God's delegation, respecting the value of every part of creation (even plants) for every other part. The message of humility and responsibility is huge, but so is the message of joy. God has declared the creation good; thus, as human stewards, we are called finally to **celebrate**!

Now we turn again to the Scripture lesson from Luke. What does this say to us about stewardship? We are tempted to ask with Peter, "Are you talking to us, Jesus?" The sayings suggest that we may be called upon to be managers and care for others; we may also be called upon to be servants, simply carrying on the master's work. Whatever work God has entrusted to us, we are capable of doing it well and capable of destroying it. In summary, we and all human beings are responsible for watchfulness (watching for God in every moment of every day), carrying on God's work, living with the expectation of God's coming, and tending God's creation according to the roles we are given. Perhaps Peter's question is answered after all. Jesus is addressing everyone—disciples and other listeners alike. We can easily read this text today as dividing the world into masters and slaves (Peter's temptation), a dangerous reading in a world that has known centuries of institutionalized slavery and still allows some people to be enslaved by economic or political or social dependence. We can also read this text as speaking to all persons, whether in leadership or worker roles or both simultaneously. We are all called to do the work we are given and to do it with expectancy that God is close at hand.

Becoming Stewards: Understanding the World

How are we to understand this world that God created? How can we be stewards without serving only human interests? Perhaps we should begin by observing one of God's smallest creatures, a squirrel. This squirrel scampers down a tall pine tree in the closing days of winter. She gathers as many dry leaves from the ground as she can hold in her small mouth; then she scampers up the low branch of one tree to the high trunk of another. When she finally nears the treetop, she slides into a hole and reappears without the leaves. She is building a nest, preparing to be fruitful and

Live in holy community:
0

Share power:

Delegate:

Celebrate:

What experiences have helped you be aware of the interdependence of all living things?

multiply. She makes the journey twenty or thirty times during one day—a great work that will provide comfort and protect the future of her children. This squirrel represents the Genesis 1 vision of creation; she simply does the work she was created to do.

As we think about what it means to be a steward, we must be careful not to distort our understanding to justify domination of God's creation or the use of creation only for human benefit. Sometimes people express concern for ecological balance, but they base their arguments solely on what is good for humans. Even when they take into account humans of succeeding generations, they may not respect the fullness of God's creation. If we are to live as faithful stewards of God's creation, we will learn from squirrels and rivers, lakes and grass. We will need to look for the revelation of God in the smallest parts of creation.

Only in the smallest revelations of God and in the fullness of *all* God's creation can we glimpse the glory of God and the very particular expectation that God has of us, namely to do the particular work that is entrusted to us. For the squirrel in late winter, that work is to gather leaves for a nest. For a person entrusted with management, that work may be to disperse food and take other responsibilities entrusted to us by the Master. For a person entrusted with service, that work is to care for the part of God's creation that is given over to our care, whether it is a child or invalid parent, a garden or neighborhood, a toxic dumping site or government program.

The division of creation into squirrels, managers, and servers is not the central point of these passages; the responsibility of each part of creation to be itself and do its unique work *is* the point. Jesus subtly communicated this to Peter when Peter wondered what messages were addressed to the intimate disciples and what messages were for everyone. Jesus' message was simple; no matter what responsibility you receive, you are to carry it forth with compassion for those beside you, with respect for the Master, and with faithfulness to the Master's ongoing work.

When we relate these ideas to our present world, we are reminded that all persons, including the poor and marginalized, are created in the image of God. We are reminded that people are to be valued, not according to their economic or social power, but simply because they are God's precious and responsible creations. We are reminded that being created in the image of God does not grant us power

to be God but power to carry on God's caring work in the world. It raises questions about genetic manipulation and abuse of land and water for human benefit. It raises questions about consumer lifestyles, in which we seek to own as much as possible and to enjoy addictions to alcohol, drugs, food, shopping, and so forth. In fact, we are reminded that all of creation is precious in God's sight. We are reminded that our basic human identity is not established by superficial achievements but by our creation in the image of God and in relationship with everything God has made. We are charged, then, to delight in God's wonders and to be faithful stewards of God's good creation.

Living in the World

In light of this analysis, how are people to live in the world? Both Genesis and Luke tell us that God holds great expectations of us. God gives people responsibility and, also, the capability and freedom to act. The downside of human capability and freedom, however, is that people often exercise their abilities for ill, or they choose freely to disobey God and abuse God's creation.

Consider where you place your faith or trust. How people understand the nature of God is important. If people trust in God as Creator and Provider, the natural response is thanksgiving. People who trust in God as Holy Community and Celebrant are drawn into relationship with the loving God who thoroughly enjoys creation. When people trust God as Power-Sharer and Delegator, they are able to receive the power and responsibility God gives. People who trust God as Master and Judge also accept responsibility, especially if these images of God are held in relationship with others and not frozen by fears of retribution.

In addition to trusting, consider other practices in your daily life. The themes of this session suggest practices that can help you grow as faithful stewards.

Creating—creating music, paintings, meals, houses, cabinets, law briefs, medical experiments, or friendships.

Creating: Reflect on what you have created in the past week, and meditate on what God is calling you to create in the next week or month.

Providing: What practices could you adopt for the coming week to provide for yourself and for those who need you, both human and non-human?	**Providing**—providing for yourself and for people, animals, plants, and lands near you or in great need. Early Methodists tended themselves and the poor because all were created in the image of God.
Holy Community: With what people and other parts of God's creation could you relate during the coming week to strengthen holy community?	**Living in holy community**—living in community with all God's creatures. St. Francis lived in community with animals and stars. Early Methodists formed into small communities to support holiness.
Sharing Power: With what parts of God's creation are you called to share power or to respect their God-given power?	**Sharing power**—sharing power with all God's creatures, respecting the power of squirrels to be squirrels, rivers to be rivers, and so forth.
Delegating: Consider what responsibilities you need to allow others to take so they can live as God intended.	**Delegating**—delegating responsibility to other creatures of God.
Celebrating: What acts of thanksgiving and celebration could you practice every day of the coming week?	**Celebrating**—celebrating the wonders of God and God's creation. With this practice, we now close, knowing that creation is very good indeed!

Steward
Living as Disciples in Everyday Life

Stewards of the Good News of Creation II

Mary Elizabeth Mullino Moore

*Read Psalm 104
Luke 12:22-34*

The theme of the previous session was creation, community, and responsibility; the theme of this session is creation, promise, and praise. Scriptures in the previous session were stories and sayings; Scriptures now are poetry. The lyrics of Psalm 104 sing with praise: "Bless the LORD, O my soul, O LORD my God, you are very great." The rhythms of Luke dance with promise: "Consider the ravens: they neither sow nor reap, they have neither storehouse nor barn, and yet God feeds them. . . . Consider the lilies, how they grow: they neither toil nor spin; yet I tell you, even Solomon in all his glory was not clothed like one of these" (Luke 12:24a, 27).

With such poetry, the invitation to be stewards of the good news of creation stirs delight and assurance. Little do we realize at first that the art of praising God and trusting God's promises is very challenging.

Stewards in Biblical Times

The singer of Psalm 104 was intoxicated with delight in God's creation. The themes are familiar from Session 2, echoing Genesis 1:1–2:4a as if the creation Scriptures were being adapted to music. In fact, Psalm 104 begins where Genesis 1 ends, underscoring God's proclamation of creation as very good (Genesis 1:31). While the psalm clearly re-sounds themes of Genesis 1, the words also remind readers of Genesis 2, the flood (Genesis 7–8), and Psalm 103 with its accent on God's mercy and reign over all creation.

In Psalm 104, we hear God described again as Creator, Provider, and Celebrant. The accent on Holy Community has shifted. Instead of the Trinity, we find God entering into community with all of creation. Elements of creation become messengers of God and collaborators in God's work. For example, the psalmist speaks to God and observes that "you make the winds your messengers, fire and flame your ministers" (Psalm 104:4). Another shift is seen in God's roles

Name some ways you experience God's presence in creation.

as Power-Sharer and Delegator; these roles are less explicit in the psalm than in Genesis, but they are pervasive from beginning to end. Grass grows for the cattle, plants for people to use, wine to gladden the human heart, oil to make the face shine, and bread to strengthen the human heart. Further, birds build their nests, mountains provide homes for wild goats, the moon marks the seasons, the sun sets at the proper time, darkness shelters the night animals in the forest, and people go to their work and labor until evening. These are only a few examples, but they illustrate well the sense of the psalmist that God has created a world in which every being has a role, and the work of every being benefits others. Each is given unique power and responsibility in creation.

The psalm is similar to Genesis 1, but the notes are not all played with the same emphasis. While Genesis 1:1–2:4*a* accents God as Power-Sharer and Delegator, the psalmist takes that for granted. While the Genesis text implies praise of God and refers to God's ongoing providence (or provision for creation), the psalmist cannot contain his or her exuberance in singing praise and embellishes grandly on God's providence. The psalm is not a creation story but a song of praise and trust in the Creator.

A word about human beings provides a transition to Luke's text. The psalmist creates a series of frames to communicate the relationships among God, creation, and human beings. The psalm begins and ends with a focus on the grandeur of God and God's work, it moves toward the center with the grandeur of God's vast creation, then it focuses on human beings in the center. This communicates a strong message, namely that the *framing* truth is God. Human beings are held in their place by the Creator God and the fullness of all creation. We live in perpetual relationship with the glory and providence of God and the multitude of God's creations.

It is interesting to note that this pattern does not hold neatly. The subject of the psalmist's song shifts rapidly, moving from people to trees to birds and lions and eventually back to people within a few verses. One senses that the psalmist, while recognizing that God calms the chaos, also recognizes the chaotic delight of God's work. Who else but God could tame the Leviathan, the symbolic and feared monster of chaos, into a playful creature? Even chaos becomes creative and good with the touch of God.

If we recognize God as the true owner of all creation, what difference would it make in the ways we live in our household?

This leads naturally to Luke's text. The flow of Luke 12:22-34 is engaging, and before we know it, we are captured by its assurances and invitation to let go of worldly cares. This, however, is one of Jesus' most subversive teachings. Luke did not include it as a comforting word to someone having a sleepless night. Luke presents this teaching between Jesus' warnings about greed (Luke 12:13-20) and his warnings about not being prepared for the Master's coming (12:35-40). All of these warnings precede the text discussed in Session 2, in which Jesus urges people to take responsibility for what the Master leaves in their charge. We see, then, that this beautiful text for Session 3 stands in hard company. It conveys much more than casual assurance to a modern reader who is feeling anxious. Jesus' sayings about ravens and lilies are uncompromising challenges to the early Christians to let go of their greed, their stockpiling of food and clothing, their striving after creature comforts, their fear. Instead the early Christians are challenged to trust God, strive for God's reign, sell their goods, give alms, and prepare for God's future. Jesus' words point to a new way of life.

...in our involvement in policy making?

Stewards in History

What is this new life, and how have Christians sought it through history? We can find as many different ways as we find Christian communities. The early Christians were not all alike. The early disciples and converts in Acts gathered together to share all things in common, give to those in need, pray in the temple, break bread at home with glad and generous hearts, praise God, and have goodwill for all people (Acts 2:43-47). Some early Christians formed into house churches, gathering for worship and service in their small communities. Some formed larger churches and struggled competitively; they debated whose religious practices were more holy and whose gifts were more important (addressed in Romans 12 and 14:1-12; 1 Corinthians 12 and 13). The early Corinthian Christians also struggled with social position; some members were tempted to eat the best food before others arrived (addressed in 1 Corinthians 11:27-34).

As time passed, Christians also formed into monastic communities, some of which emphasized simple living. For

...in our care of ourselves?

Saint Francis and the Franciscan community, simple living was accompanied with praise, as witnessed in Francis's own song of praise composed on his pain-ridden deathbed. You will hear it in the video. Other religious communities emphasized equality and shared responsibility, as in monastic communities of early Celtic Ireland where abbots and abbesses, brothers and sisters, lived in close collaboration with one another and with the earth.

Even as the church became identified with the dominant political authority of the Roman Empire and even as it amassed great power and wealth over the ensuing centuries, people in many villages, homes, monasteries, and city streets continued to center their lives on praising God. Some of their stories are legendary.

The sixteenth and seventeenth centuries marked major shifts in the church, leading to the Reformation with its emerging Protestant churches and simultaneous reforms within Roman Catholicism. This was a very difficult time in which Christians turned against Christians and changes were emerging with much pain and more than a little violence. People, however, sought to return to central Christian values; they sought to understand and follow the new life to which Jesus had pointed. During this era, John Calvin wrote eloquently of God's creation and identified the chief aim of human beings to glorify God and do God's work. During this era, the Anabaptists emerged, standing *against* culture and standing *for* what they understood as the most fundamental values of God. Arising from the Anabaptist movement were Amish and Mennonite communities, who, to this day, seek to witness for peace and simplicity in a larger culture of war and extravagance.

In what ways do you think God is calling you to use the gifts you have been given?

Within the Wesleyan heritage, John Wesley saw God as the source of all good gifts. Early Methodists gave themselves to holy living, trusting that only God can save but that God can save no matter how far people fall. Early Wesleyan practices included singing praise whenever people gathered, and we find dominant themes of praise and thanksgiving in Charles Wesley's hymns. Followers of the Wesleys built simple chapels and preaching halls rather than lavish churches, seeking to keep people within the Church of England and avoiding competitive, extravagant living. We find among early Methodists the rough and unpopular practices of reaching out to poor coal miners and farmers,

preaching in fields, living close to the hard experiences of life, and yet turning to God with trust and hope.

Through history, we see people seeking to live into the promise of God, who has created and provided, while trusting and praising God, who continues to create and care for creation throughout time. The church has fallen short, but people, in their many distinctive ways, have continued to strive toward God's promises for God's future.

Stewards in Our Time

How do these promises engage us today? The two biblical texts for this session are filled with promise, but they are also intimidating. How does God provide? What is this providence upon which creation can depend? Can we still depend upon it? These questions are urgent in a world of consumerism where people form their self-worth around what they own, what jobs they hold, how others value them. One is tempted to say that the Scriptures hark back to a simpler time when simplicity was easy, when praise of God and trust in God's work were as natural as sleeping and waking. But consider how people in biblical times were tempted again and again to place their values outside of God and godliness. Consider how Christian leaders through the centuries called people back to values of love and justice and righteousness.

The world in which we live is very different from the world of the psalmist or the world of Luke, but some qualities are similar. We, like them, live in troubled times where wars rage, one nation dominates another, people compete for glory and wealth, people are tempted by flashy toys and superficial honors, one ethnic community judges itself superior to others, and people value their own religious and ethical beliefs over the God to whom those beliefs point. How can the Bible help with these dilemmas? The texts of this session turn us first to God.

In Psalm 104, God is **creating** (making) again and again, and God's creating continues long after the world was first made. Consider one example: "You make springs gush forth in the valleys; they flow between the hills, giving drink to every wild animal. . . . From your lofty abode you water the mountains; the earth is satisfied with the fruit of your work" (Psalm 104:10-13; cf. 104:29-31). The psalmist, here and elsewhere, sees God as continuing to create, working on

Name some ways that God continues creating...

providing sustenance . . .

providing delight . . .

providing hospitality . . .

teaching . . .

behalf of creation to provide **sustenance**. This ongoing care that God gives creation is one reason this psalm is often read at Pentecost; it is a declaration of God's Spirit moving throughout creation—in the earliest creating days, in the birthing of the Christian church, and even in our present day. Note too that God provides more than basic sustenance. God also provides for **delight** ("wine to gladden the human heart") and for **hospitality** ("oil to make the face shine," hospitality of trees for birds, hospitality of mountains for wild goats, and hospitality of darkness for night creatures). In sum, God's providential care covers the basic necessities of life and far more!

In the tumultuous world in which we live, the psalmist promises human beings and the rest of creation just such care—continuing creation, sustenance in basic necessities, delight, and hospitality. With the ozone layer becoming thinner, the rainforests becoming more threatened, and species of plants and animals going out of existence every day, one wonders if God is still providing. The promise is there, however, and springs do still gush forth in the valleys. Environmentalists are tempted to speak as prophets of doom. The psalmist, however, invites stewards of God's creation to begin with praise not doom.

Perhaps that is the more difficult and promising road. Dwelling on the threat of disaster often freezes people to nonaction. Dwelling on the providence of God and the goodness of God's creation promises to inspire, challenge, and empower people to sing to God and live with hope: "May the glory of the LORD endure forever; may the LORD rejoice in his works" (104:31). This is not a passive waiting for God to act but an active praising and meditating that has power to reshape our priorities and ways of living. This is not an ignoring of trouble either. The psalmist closes with hope that the psalm itself ("my meditation") will be pleasing to God and that sinners and wickedness will be removed from the earth. The refrain, thus, does not ignore the presence of evil but seeks not to dwell on it as the central issue. Sin and wickedness are not simple problems that people can fix; the choice, instead, is to pour energy into glorifying God. Thus, the psalm ends as it began: "Bless the LORD, O my soul. Praise the LORD!"

The plot thickens when we turn to Luke. Here Jesus is not creating but **teaching**. Consider his series of admonitions in verses 22-34: "do not worry about your life," "consider the

ravens," "consider the lilies," "do not keep striving," "strive for God's kingdom," "do not be afraid," "sell your possessions, and give alms," and "make purses for yourselves that do not wear out." This amazing list does not instruct people to neglect daily life. Remember the first creation story and Jesus' instructions for managers and servers in the previous session. Responsibility is paramount, but God and God's creation are even more so. Human responsibility exists in a frame of God's providence and good creation. Thus, we are urged to take responsibility, but we are also urged not to worry or strive for earthly splendor. We are invited to learn from the ravens and lilies and to strive for *God's* future.

Although most modern people no longer hold the early church's expectation that God will end the world tomorrow or the next day, we do live with awareness that humans are capable of destroying the world or large portions of it on any given day. We also live with promises of God's reign and the call to live toward it. How would the modern world be different if people asked themselves every morning, "What could I do today to prepare for God's new creation?"

Becoming Stewards: Understanding the World

How are we to understand this world that God created? The ideas we have considered thus far are countercultural! Luke seems to be asking the impossible, and the ancient psalm stands in sharp contrast with contemporary culture. Consider modern images of human life: **clever people** who have almost unlimited capacity to create and solve problems; **consumer people** who receive goods and services from creation's vast supply; **self-righteous people** who proclaim how the world is plunging into destruction (whether because of drugs, political wrong-headedness, ecological abuse, religious distortions, or other problems); **isolationist people** who are charged to care for their own and let the rest of creation care for itself; and **self-sufficient people** who have no need to learn from others. These dominant cultural views transcend religious divisions; they are not unique to so-called liberals *or* conservatives. They even transcend social classes, ethnic communities, and other human differences.

Certainly, celebrating God and God's creation and letting go of worries seem like naïve answers to complex, modern

Write your own poem or prayer of praise to God.

problems. But answers echo off the walls of our biblical texts, and they inspire the following poem, "Bless you, O God." Poetry may be the only way to speak of such things.

> Bless you, O God!
> As I gaze from your mountaintops,
> I see largesse in your creation,
>> spreading far beyond the far horizons where my
>> eyes travel.
> I see the flutter of birds' wings,
>> graceful movements of a deer,
>> gentle bubbling of a mountain stream,
>>> sweeping down rocks and fallen trees to the
>>> valleys below,
>>> while fish swim and hide and play,
>> a soft carpet of leaves and nuts and needles,
>>> waiting their time to soak into the earth and
>>> give birth once more,
>> a roaring waterfall, giving witness to powers great—
>>> powers that bring life from chaos
>>> and creation from that which frightens us most!
>
> Bless you, O God!
> As I gaze across your ocean depths,
> I see infinity in your creation,
>> reaching around the earth
>> and plunging to the deepest depths of the earth's
>> core.
> I see fish swimming and dolphins leaping,
>> whales making their long journeys
>>> to places where their bodies know they must
>>> go,
>> golden seaweed flowing and mysterious coral
>> growing,
>> rising waves,
>>> revealing the thinnest top of the ocean's
>>> massive movements,
>> glaciers rising into the sky,
>>> pointing to cold mysteries too large to see,
>>> too strong to name.
>
> Bless you, O God!
> As I walk across your earth,
> I feel the tenderness and intricacy of your creation,

I hear the mating of animals,
 see the budding of trees,
 smell the winds that blow from north and south,
  east and west,
 carrying pollen and grain to make new life in new
   homes,
 taste the moisture of your breath,
  which will soon fall as rain and snow to water
   the land.
I feel your creation all around me,
 tending itself as you intended,
 sometimes failing, sometimes hurting, often dying,
 but always rekindling into new life
 under the steady care of your fingers,
 the watchful attention of your spirit,
 the tender compassion of your being.
In the midst of your creation,
 I am ever so small,
 ever so well cared for,
 ever so blessed;
My soul longs only for you,
 when I let go of my fear
 and give myself to living
  and singing your praise,
Bless you, O God!

Living in the World

In light of the analysis and poetry in this session, how are people to live in the world? How might people participate in God's work of creating, sustaining creation, delighting in every spark of life, offering hospitality to God's vast creation, and learning from the ravens and lilies? Below are some practices to guide your decisions.

Praising—If God is Creator, you and I are called to praise God for the wonders of this earth.

Praising: During the next week, choose a time each day to sit quietly and write a list of all the gifts of creation for which you are thankful. Be aware of moments when you actually praised God (silently or aloud); identify new opportunities to say thanks.

Receiving: Identify at least one way that you could let go of a heavy worry or extravagance during the coming week or month; how might this create space for you to give attention to those who need it most?

Receiving God's care and sustaining others—If God provides for sustenance, you and I are called to receive and be thankful—receive the blessings of rain and sun, human companionship, laughter and tears. We are also invited to sustain others—let go of worry and excessive possessions, give alms, give ourselves. Ironically, one of the best ways to let go of our own worries and excesses is to show concern for others.

Delighting: Set aside one particular time in the next week when you can engage in pure enjoyment, whether in a special meal, a party, a quiet evening with someone special, a walk, or some other joy-filled activity. At the end of every day, meditate on the moments of joy in that particular day.

Delighting in the world—If God delights in creation and provides delight for all created beings, you and I are called to enjoy—to delight in God and the things of God.

Hospitality: Name one way in which you can offer hospitality in the next week to some part of God's creation. Consider personal and larger political action options.

Receiving and giving hospitality—If God provides hospitality in creation, we are called to receive graciously. In a time of meditation, be aware that the earth is your home, spread before you by God; be aware also that the earth is home to all God's creatures.

Learning from others—If God is our teacher, you and I are called to learn from God's Scriptures, creatures (ravens and lilies), and presence in the ongoing movement of creation.

Learning: Study the complexities of one ecological concern, and work with a group in developing and implementing an action plan to address that concern.

In a more meditative way, spend silent time with a non-human part of God's creation. Open yourself to this gift of creation; be thankful for what it teaches you! And thank God!

Suggestions for Further Reading

Berry, Wendell. *Sex, Economy, Freedom & Community: Eight Essays*, New York: Pantheon Books, 1994.

Heywood, W., ed. *The Little Flowers of St. Francis of Assisi*. Vintage Spiritual Classics. New York: Vintage Books, 1998.

McDaniel, Jay Byrd. *With Roots and Wings: Christianity in an Age of Ecology and Dialogue*. Ecology and Justice. Maryknoll, N.Y.: Orbis Books, 1995.

McDonagh, Sean. *The Greening of the Church*. Maryknoll, N.Y.: Orbis Books, 1990.

Moore, Mary Elizabeth. *Ministering with the Earth*. St. Louis: Chalice Press, 1998. (See particularly chapters 2 and 3.)

Thistlethwaite, Susan Brooks, and Mary Potter Engel, ed. *Lift Every Voice: Constructing Christian Theologies from the Underside*. Maryknoll, N.Y.: Orbis Books, 1998.

Quinn, Frederick. *To Heal the Earth: A Theology of Ecology*. Nashville: Upper Room Books, 1994.

Rasmussen, Larry L. *Earth Community, Earth Ethics*. Maryknoll, N.Y.: Orbis Books, 1998.

Van Dyke, Fred et al., *Redeeming Creation: The Biblical Basis for Environmental Stewardship*. Westmont, Ill.: InterVarsity Press, 1996.

Walsh, James; Jean LeClercq; and Edmund Colledge, ed. *Julian of Norwich Showings*. Princeton: Princeton University Press, 1997.

Also of interest:

Global Action Plan for the Earth (GAP), www.globalactionplan.org was founded in 1989 as a nonprofit education organization. GAP supports the development of environmentally sustainable lifestyles worldwide. Over the past 10 years, GAP has developed an effective neighborhood–organizing model in its work with over 15,000 people and hundreds of neighborhood groups through the U.S.

Web of Creation, www.webofcreation.org, is an ecumenical Web site exploring eco-justice issues and advocacy from a faith perspective. It includes suggested resources, a calendar of events, and ways to involve children.

Stewards of the Good News of Faith Communities I

V. Sue Zabel
In consultation with Bishop Alfred Johnson

Read   Exodus 19:4-6
1 Corinthians
12:4-13

One of the great gifts that God has given us is the gift of community. We find this gift in many places—in our families, in our neighborhoods, in the groups we form and join that share common purpose and commitment. One of the most important communities that God has given us is the church—the body of Christ. This is the place where we are challenged and supported in our daily attempts to live as faithful disciples of Jesus Christ. This week and next we will think together about our faith communities and the ways that we can be God's stewards of our life together.

●●●

Christian communities are the contemporary stewards or caretakers of the ancient promises made between God and God's people. In Exodus 19, God initiates a covenant relationship with the Hebrew people. Out of the saving acts in Exodus and Resurrection, God raised up a community of people to be partners in the ongoing work of redemption in the world. As inheritors of this covenant tradition, Christian communities today are called to be stewards of a tradition that challenges the often self-serving values of the world around us and calls us to live righteously and justly.

God blesses us with abundant gifts for this faith journey. In 1 Corinthians 12, Paul enumerates the spiritual gifts that each member of Christ's body is given for the building up of God's whole community. Each member, especially the less prominent, is essential for the work of the body that God intends. We are stewards of these spiritual gifts given not for our personal benefit alone but for the good of the community.

As at Mt. Sinai and in Corinth, God still invites people to be stewards of the covenant and to be transformed in the life of the Spirit to which they are called.

Stewards in Biblical Times

Living as Covenant People

Exodus 19 describes God's initiation of a special relationship, the covenant, with the Hebrew people. God's covenant with the Hebrew people redefined the conventional legal contract into a mutual but unequal partnership. As sovereign, God could have demanded unquestioning subservience. Instead God offered the Hebrew people a choice: "If you obey my voice and keep my covenant, you shall be my treasured possession out of all the peoples" (Exodus 19:5).

A recurrent pattern is visible in God's relationship with the Hebrew people:

Situation of distress→Unexpected deliverance→Response in community.[1]

God enlisted Moses to lead the Hebrew people out of slavery and bondage in Egypt, a situation of intolerable *distress*. At the wilderness of Sinai, as the people camped in the valley, Moses went up the mountain, and God instructed Moses to remind the Hebrew people that "I bore you on eagles' wings and brought you to myself" (19:4).

Consistently holy, loving, gracious, steadfast, and just, God dramatically and *unexpectedly delivered* the people from oppression, bearing them up "on eagles' wings," and rescuing them from Pharaoh's advancing army. Then, as the liberated people wandered in the wilderness, God initiated through Moses a covenant to show the way to live faithfully with God and with each other. Out of a dispirited situation, God calls forth new life in *community*.

God surprises us. "Out of all the peoples," God picked unlikely partners—a people oppressed in Egypt by Pharaoh, former slaves, and exiles who were wandering in the wilderness. God entrusted the covenant to a group of displaced immigrants.

When Moses came back down the mountain and recited "all these words that the LORD had commanded," the people immediately responded, "Everything that the LORD has spoken we will do" (19:7-8). Essentially, they blindly signed a blank check! Perhaps God's yet-unknown ten commands held less terror than returning to Pharaoh. For whatever reason, they proclaimed their obedience.

After they agreed to keep the covenant, God instructed Moses to consecrate the people. Only then did God provide the terms of the covenant: the Ten Commandments (Exodus 20).

God's commandments provide the framework of the Hebrew people's response to God. Though they address issues in daily life rather than disembodied abstractions, the ten commands do not provide precise prescriptions for living in community as a holy people. Wrestling with these commandments and what they mean today occurs again and again in the community of faith.

The covenant story accents God's choice of ordinary people as a precious privilege. If God could trust this motley crew of wanderers, God must trust us and think we are able to be "a priestly kingdom and a holy nation" to carry out God's mission in the world. Nevertheless, those God chooses to be "my treasured possession out of all the peoples" also carry a heavier burden of responsibility.

What is our part in the covenant?

In order to fulfill God's covenant, the Hebrew people were equipped with particular gifts that they were expected to contribute for the benefit of the whole community. Moses' father-in-law, Jethro, confronted Moses for trying to do everything himself. Jethro advised Moses, "You will surely wear yourself out, both you and these people with you. For the task is too heavy for you; you cannot do it alone" (18:18). Following his advice, Moses appointed wise, capable arbiters to oversee the decisions of smaller, manageably sized groups. God commissioned Aaron and his descendants to be Israel's priests. For the construction of the tabernacle and its furnishings, God called forth artisans. As the biblical account unfolded, God lifted up judges, kings and queens, prophets, musicians, farmers, midwives, healers, mystics, teachers, leaders, administrators, miracle-workers, interpreters, persons extending hospitality, warriors, and peacemakers.

Living as Christ's Body

The convental pattern found in Exodus 19 has parallels in the New Testament.

Situation of distress→Unexpected deliverance→Response in community.[1]

What does God's covenant with humanity have to say about our life as a congregation?

Jesus experienced the horrible distress of death on the cross, the *unexpected deliverance* from death through resurrection, and the response of the new *community*.

The people in the church at Corinth quarreled and were in *distress*, divided over several issues: Who among them is the most important and powerful? How should the church deal with immorality? What constitutes right worship? And which spiritual gifts are superior? Paul reminded them that Jesus Christ died and was resurrected to *deliver* them from sin and death, "God is faithful; by him you were called into the fellowship of his Son, Jesus Christ our Lord" (1 Corinthians 1:9).

New life in Christ Jesus is new life in *community*. Paul stressed the Corinthians' unity in Christ. "In the one Spirit we were all baptized into one body" (12:13)—Jews, Greeks, slaves, free, men, women. By God's grace, members of the church at Corinth manifested a profusion of spiritual gifts intended for the good of the whole body of Christ. Paul explains, "There are varieties of gifts, but the same Spirit; and there are varieties of services, but the same Lord; and there are varieties of activities, but it is the same God who activates all of them in everyone" (12:4-6). God, Lord, and Spirit are one and the source of the gifts, services, and activities needed for the common good to the glory of God.

Where have you experienced God's grace in your life?

In 1 Corinthians 12:12-31, Paul compared the church with the human body. The analogy of society with the body was a common rhetorical metaphor in the ancient world. Paul reworked the metaphor to accentuate interdependence and unity. Instead of admonishing the subordinate classes to stay in their place, as was a common use of the image, Paul underscored the value of all contributors to the Christian community, regardless of their social or spiritual status. He boldly claimed, "God has so arranged the body, giving the greater honor to the inferior member" (12:24*b*). The community, like a body, requires diversity to function and flourish.

Paul adds another twist to the body metaphor—*you*, the church at Corinth, *are* the body of Christ. As the body of Christ, members are given diverse gifts of the Spirit for the healthy functioning of the whole community. Examples include apostleship, prophecy, teaching, deeds of power, healing, forms of assistance, leadership, and tongues.

The Spirit and gifts of the Spirit are available in overflowing abundance to all. Since the body requires diversity and interdependence, there is then no basis for divisions among the members. In unity all care, suffer, and rejoice together. There is no place for domination of

privileged individuals or groups over others. Throughout the Bible, the faithful are called to care for anyone who has need or is marginal in the community, even to give them special recognition.

Stewards in History

With organizational abilities akin to Moses and Paul, John Wesley, the founder of Methodism, was also a master at coordinating the body for the work of ministry. Wesley sought to revitalize a languishing Church of England during the eighteenth century, a time of revolutionary social, economic, and technological change. Beginning during his school years at Oxford, he organized his companions into a holy club for systematic Bible study, mutual discipline in devotion, and frequent Eucharist. They regularly visited prisoners and assisted poor families.

Wesley preached about a God who loves and seeks to be in relationship with all human beings. The new life in Christ described in 1 Corinthians is available to all who will receive God's forgiveness, acceptance, and love. Through grace, we are given spiritual gifts to turn our lives around, keep the covenant with God, and do all the good that we can in Christ's name.

Wesley's spiritual gifts of preaching, leadership, and evangelism soon attracted followers, and a revival movement was initiated in England and in the American colonies. Disregarded by the hierarchy and nominal members of the Church of England, Wesley preached in open fields to the working poor and destitute. Many were poorly educated or illiterate. As the crowds grew, he organized lay preachers to assist him with preaching and oversight of small groups of the people called Methodist.

Jethro advised Moses to systematically organize the Hebrews to assist him. Similarly, Wesley organized followers into small groups for the purpose of mutual nurture, growing maturity in faith, and pastoral care. Leaders facilitated "watching over one another in love" and collected contributions to be distributed to the needy. Members were expected to continue to worship in the Church of England and regularly receive Eucharist.

Wesley believed personal faith is inextricably related to life in community. Similar to Paul's admonitions to the Corinthians, Wesley expected Christians to employ their

In what ways can you be an instrument of God's grace?

In what ways can your congregation be an instrument of God's grace?

spiritual gifts to build up the community. If Christians practice their faith daily by attending to personal devotion and acts of compassion such as forgiveness, tolerance, and generosity toward others, Wesley expected that transformation of individuals, the church, and society would follow.

Wesley's ministry was with the poor and voiceless people. He did not talk about impoverishment or oppression in the abstract. Compassion and justice require first-hand knowledge, understanding, and involvement. Wesley stressed the importance of visiting the sick, poor, and imprisoned. He opposed slavery, war, and the exploitation of the poor. He advocated adequate health care, housing, and education for the poor and their children. He believed that loving God meant following God's commandment to love and serve one's neighbors. In so doing, we become friends with Christ.

Wesley's class meeting can be a useful model for us today. The weekly meeting opened with prayer and brief hymn singing. In a question-and-answer format, the leader invited each class member to give an accounting of her or his life and relationship with Christ since the last meeting. There were two purposes: for class members to unburden themselves and to realize that they were not alone in their struggles and doubts. Sharing of their life stories, with their sorrows and joys, was intended to be instructive. The meeting concluded with prayer and singing of a hymn. Over time members came to trust one another and "watch over one another in love."

Stewards in Our Time

What spiritual gifts has God given to you?

By virtue of our baptism, all Christians are called to ministry in Christ's name. For the work of ministry within the body of Christ, everyone is given gifts that are discerned spiritually (1 Corinthians 2:12-14). These vocational gifts equip members of the body for particular callings and are exercised in community not in isolation. *Charis* (spiritual gifts) are "the power of the resurrected Christ at work in those who are joined to Christ through baptism (1 Corinthians 12:6, 11). All of the baptized are 'office-bearers,' and each has a charism or power and the responsibility to exercise that gift for the good of others (1 Corinthians 14)."[2]

Spiritual gifts are not intended for exclusive use within congregations. These ministries may be expressed corporately on behalf of the church or individually in secular employment, volunteer commitments, and family, as well as church-related endeavors. The world needs committed Christians who live their faith in all kinds of vocational callings.

As with the Hebrew people who could accept or reject the covenant initiated in Exodus, God still gives us the radical freedom to say no. Rather than contribute our spiritual gifts for the good of community as God intends, we can reject our gifts, allow them to remain dormant, or employ them for selfish gain and detriment.

Following the Spirit should bring delight and joy! Frederick Buechner describes what it means to be called by God and to use one's spiritual gifts vocationally:

> There are all different kinds of voices calling you to all different kinds of work, and the problem is to find out which is the voice of God rather than of Society, say, or the Superego, or Self-Interest.

> By and large a good rule for finding out is this. The kind of work God usually calls you to is the kind of work (a) that you need most to do and (b) that the world most needs to have done . . .

> The place God calls you to is the place where your deep gladness and the world's deep hunger meet.[3]

Which of your gifts give you the most "deep gladness?"

People are looking for this kind of deep gladness and meaning in their lives. Earning more and consuming more does not satisfy our spiritual longings. Increasingly, individuals and groups are seeking ways to make a difference. Faith communities that open their doors to new people and new possibilities for mission can be a catalyst for spiritual renewal in Christ's name. Imagine the release of creativity and energy that would be generated if the spiritual gifts and ministry of all baptized Christians were seriously recognized and authorized! Imagine lay members and clergy engaging in mutual partnership with one another as they carry out the mission of the church in the world.

The church has previous experience with revitalization through the deployment of laity for ministry. John Wesley

What spiritual gifts are active in your congregation?

launched a renewal of the church with lay preachers and lay leaders. He incurred the hostility of established clergy and church leaders who were threatened by a potential shift of power. Despite their opposition, the movement grew. Wesley did not do away with the traditions and practices of the church. Quite the contrary—he emphasized Bible reading, prayer, fasting, regular attendance in worship, frequent Eucharist, and charity.

Lively, energetic congregations are experiencing similar renewal today when they are open to new ways of empowering and coordinating ministry for the good of the community and world. Spirited congregations are already shifting to ministries based on each person's gifts rather than official church position or hierarchical committees.

Defining ministries based on the world's deep need linked with members' spiritual gifts requires reordering the way most congregations organize themselves for ministry. No single pattern of organization guarantees instant fruition or even long-range success. In fact, change can be initially disorienting as new ways of following the Spirit's lead are discerned.

The church is experiencing a transition away from official, professional leadership to gifts-based leadership. People and their spiritual gifts are becoming the primary focus rather than programs and positions. Looser, innovative congregational structures are emerging that replace rigid bureaucratic models with fluid task- and project-oriented patterns for ministry. As a body, each congregation can define their particular, corporate spiritual gifts that they contribute to the neighborhood and global communities.

What deep needs are visible in your community?

Moses led the Hebrew people through a disorienting wilderness transition into God's promised future in a new land. The Corinthians to whom Paul preached and wrote lived in a time of societal turmoil and transition. The environment in which the church ministers today is undergoing major paradigm shifts. These changes call for new ways of being in ministry.

Identification of each person's and each faith community's call to ministry and the spiritual gifts that they bring to that ministry can be a unifying theme for congregation renewal. In all aspects of life, each person has an opportunity to serve as partners in God's ongoing creative and redemptive work in the world.

Becoming Stewards: Understanding the World

God entrusted the covenant to the Hebrew immigrants who overcame staggering obstacles to create a new life in a new land. Some members of the Corinthian church were immigrants or their descendants. Colonists who were former slaves (Roman freedmen) had moved to this Near Eastern commercial crossroads seeking a better life and upward mobility. Gifts of the Spirit were distributed among members of the Corinthian church, including these Gentile converts.

Our perspectives about these situations are different depending on where we are situated in our economic, political, or social system. Those who are relatively comfortable in their economic and social world may view the church as charitable and humane. Those at the margins, however, may perceive church members as do-gooders who systematically exclude them from full and meaningful participation.

A round table is the image of church where all are welcomed, have a place, and can speak their distinctive voice. Perhaps the familiar potluck church supper is the perfect metaphor for spiritual gifts—all contribute their specialty to the table. There is plenty for all. We can look at and touch one another as we talk about our lives.

It is not enough to wait for people to show up at God's welcoming table. To be God's holy, righteous, and just covenant people means going out into the streets and unlikely places in our communities to search and recruit those whom society has hidden and excluded. Full participation at the table requires holistic attention to each guest's spiritual, physical, social, economic, and psychological well-being.

As God's covenant community and as members of Christ's body, the common good necessitates inclusion of each member's gifts for ministry. We are called to the partnership God covenanted with us—not pitying beneficence. Thus, Jesus' followers are called to use their spiritual gifts in ways that also call forth others' gifts and correct whatever impedes everyone's contribution to the life of the community, including attitudes, relationships, or social structures.

Where is God calling you to respond to those deep needs?

Living in the World

Write a statement that describes your covenant with God regarding your life.

Think about your life and the events in your community. Where is God active? Can you identify evidence of God *unexpectedly delivering* you, other individuals, or large and small groups from situations of distress and the emerging new community that results?

How would you describe your agreement with God regarding your life? Write a statement that describes your covenant. What does it mean to be holy today?

Reflect on your stewardship of your unique gifts to the community. You might contribute your gifts with family, church-related activities, employment, and volunteer work. Is the Spirit leading you in new directions? Is God calling you to a new expression of your Christian vocation? What steps do you need to take to realize God's call on your life?

Individually or in a group, assess your own covenant with God in the areas of compassion, justice, worship, and devotion. Are some areas neglected or out of balance? What might you do to strengthen your own discipleship?

John Wesley frequently conducted covenant services when he visited the Methodist societies. An adaptation of his service is found in *The United Methodist Book of Worship* and various forms have been used in a variety of denominations. If it is not already a part of your congregation's practices, introduce the service in conjunction with New Year's celebrations.

In what ways is your congregation responding to the world's deep hungers?

Who is included and excluded from the round table in your congregation? As a part of a special study or strategic planning process, analyze who are active members and the ways they put their spiritual gifts into practice for ministry. Then investigate who is absent from the table. Whose gifts are overlooked? Undertake a congregational study in which you determine the needs of the community where the church is located. Your assessment might include demographics, interviews, history, culture, social and economic dynamics, and other environmental factors affecting congregational and community life. As the world's deep hungers are raised to consciousness, what is the particular calling of your congregation? What spiritual gifts can it gladly and uniquely bring to help satisfy those hungers?

Engage in an assessment of spiritual gifts through a process of discernment, surrender, celebration, and creative

action. The list at the end of Session 5 contains resources to help you do this. When we use this kind of process we find that we do not focus on filling positions on committees or an organizational chart. Instead ministry is organized to connect the world's deep needs with the spiritual gifts of the church and its members. Reorganizing for ministry is no small undertaking but can revitalize congregations to become more faithful stewards of God's covenant and of the spiritual gifts with which we have been blessed.

1. Bruce C. Birch, *Let Justice Roll Down: The Old Testament, Ethics, and Christian Life* (Louisville: Westminster John Knox Press, 1991), p. 131.

2. Letty M. Russell, *Church in the Round: Feminist Interpretation of the Church* (Louisville: Westminster John Knox Press, 1993), p. 66.

3. Frederick Buechner, *Wishful Thinking: A Theological ABC* (New York: Harper & Row, 1973), p. 95.

Stewards of the Good News of Faith Communities II

V. Sue Zabel
In consultation with Bishop Alfred Johnson

The song of the unfruitful vineyard found in Isaiah 5:1-7 and the discussion of spiritual gifts in 1 Corinthians 12 depict situations in which God's people flounder in their efforts to be faithful followers. In both texts, individual aggrandizement prevails over the good of the community. In Isaiah, instead of finding righteousness and justice, God grieves over bloodshed and the cries of the oppressed. In 1 Corinthians, Paul instructs a community of faith in which God's spiritual gifts have been flagrantly distorted. Instead of using their spiritual gifts for the good of the community, some members of the Corinthian church flaunted them in worship as signs of their personal spiritual superiority.

As in Session 4, these Scripture passages make it clear that personal and social transformation must go hand in hand. God graciously blesses us with spiritual gifts. Throughout the Bible, we are commanded to exercise those gifts as God's partners in such a way that our devotion and worship is always linked with compassion and justice.

Read Isaiah 5:1-9
1 Corinthians
12: 14-31

What does the parable Isaiah tells have to say about our life together as a community of faith?

Stewards in Biblical Times

The book of Isaiah is a literary presentation of the sayings of the prophet Isaiah. Biblical prophets were inspired persons who presented a word of God to the often stubborn and unfaithful Hebrew people. Isaiah 5:1-7, called the song of the unfruitful vineyard, is a parable about God's disappointment over the failure of the covenant community to be "a priestly kingdom and a holy nation" (Exodus 19:6). The parable begins with the prophet Isaiah assuming the role of a lover singing to the beloved. In a dramatic twist in verse 3, the parable becomes a prophetic indictment of God's people for failing to follow God's standards of justice and righteousness.

Initially the singer (the prophet) was the friend and advocate for his companion, God, and, in the beginning, sang about God's unrequited love for the vineyard. The metaphor of the vineyard can be understood in multiple ways. In Isaiah 5:1, the depiction of the vineyard signaled that the poem was a love song, since the image of the vineyard was a standard metaphor for love in Israelite love poetry (such as Song of Songs). The metaphor of the vineyard was also a common figure of speech signifying God's people. In addition, vineyards were a common indication of agricultural wealth and a sign of God's blessing.

By verse 3, the prophet-singer unexpectedly exited, and the owner of the vineyard, God, directly expressed judgment of Israel and Judah. God lamented, "What more was there to do for my vineyard that I have not done in it?" God had lovingly selected a fertile field, cleared the stones, built a watchtower, and planted the choicest plants. And what did God get for all this effort—not lush growth but wild grapes! God has finally had it—the field will be allowed to go to waste.

A crucial word play in verse 7 is a pivotal clue for understanding the meaning of Isaiah 5. God looked for justice (*mishpat*) but found bloodshed (*mispach*). God sought righteousness (*tsedaqah*) but heard a cry (*tse'aqah*), the cry of the oppressed. The good that God originally intended in the covenant with the Hebrew people was terribly distorted. The rest of Isaiah 5 (verses 8-24), graphically enumerates Israel and Hudah's crimes of injustice and bloodshed, the consequences of defeat by the Assyrians, and the subsequent exile of the Israelites. Just as it was to the inhabitants of Jerusalem and Judah, the song of the unfruitful vineyard is another reminder that faithful stewards of God's covenant are expected to be just and righteous.

First Corinthians was written to another faith community that distorted God's gifts, in this case, for personal glorification. The problem Paul addressed in 1 Corinthians 12–14 was that some Corinthian Christians boasted about their showy, disorderly, and self-centered worship practices and disrupted the unity of the newly formed Christian community. Some members of the various house churches in Corinth flaunted manifestations of their spiritual gifts, especially speaking in tongues, and competed over whose spiritual gifts were superior.

Paul admonished the Corinthians that every spiritual gift was a result of God's free, unmerited grace for all.

What do you think Paul might say to your congregation today?

Distributed in diverse ways to everyone, none of the spiritual gifts was a private possession. Paul stressed, "To each is given the manifestation of the Spirit for the common good" (1 Corinthians 12:7). Therefore, no one should consider his or her spiritual gift superior to others.

Manifestations of extraordinary, divinely inspired spiritual gifts have a single source—God. In 1 Corinthians 12:4-6, Paul used three designations for God—Spirit, Lord, God— and linked them with three overlapping ways God works in the church—gifts (*charismata*), services (*diakoniai*), and activities (*energemata*).

In verses 8-10, Paul gave examples of the diversity of spiritual gifts: wisdom, knowledge, faith, healing, working of miracles, prophecy, discernment of spirits, tongues, and interpretation of tongues. The list is not exhaustive. There are several listings of spiritual gifts in the Bible—none exactly alike. In addition to those listed in 1 Corinthians 12:6-8, the main passages include 1 Corinthians 12:27-30, Romans 12:6-8, 1 Peter 4:10-11, and Ephesians 4:11-13.

The gift of speaking in tongues was a particularly sensitive source of tension for the Corinthian Christians. In the ancient world, arcane "angelic" speech (such as speaking in tongues) was sometimes considered a mark of sophisticated spirituality and privileged status. Consequently, the Corinthian Christians who spoke in tongues may have also claimed special knowledge that set them apart from or above the rest of the community. Throughout 1 Corinthians, Paul reprimanded these boastful members about their domineering and arrogant practices.

Name some people you know who are using their spiritual gifts to build up the community.

Stewards in History

Throughout history, numerous faithful forefathers and foremothers have employed their particular spiritual gifts in ministries for the edification of the body of Christ. In public and private arenas, they witnessed God's love for all people. These practical theologians have wisdom to share about their stewardship of their spiritual gifts and daily practices of justice and righteousness.

Christian practices are the "things Christian people do together over time in response to and in the light of God's active presence for the life of the world."[1] Some of these practices are part of the "big picture" of the ongoing tradition of the church. Other practices represent the "little"

ways faith is expressed in daily life. As we pay close attention to Christian practices, we may begin to notice how our ordinary lives are intertwined with what God is doing in the world. Two exemplary stories from our history help us claim new possibilities for our present.

Saint Martin de Porres: A "Little Story" from History

What are some "little stories" about people in your congregation or community?

Saint Martin de Porres is an example of how the spiritual gifts of an unlikely person are used for God's purposes. The "little stories" about relatively unknown Christians are usually found in poems, stories, and songs. The simplicity of these "little stories" about people like Saint. Martin de Porres reveal profound spiritual truths. They may also expose injustices. In the case of Saint. Martin de Porres, "little stories" unmask the racism of the church toward indigenous persons of mixed blood.[2]

Saint Martin de Porres was a Dominican mulatto saint who was born in Lima, Peru, in 1575 and died in 1639. People from all races and power groups recognized his sainthood during his lifetime, yet he was not canonized until 1962. Saint Martin de Porres was the son of the Spanish Don Juan de Porres and the freed black slave Ana Velazquez. Though he did not make it publicly known that he had a mulatto son, Don Juan apprenticed Martin to a barber. In the sixteenth century in Peru, barbers did more than cut hair—they provided medical treatments, especially to the common people. Martin soon gained a reputation for healing people whom other doctors had given up for dead. He also treated cats and dogs.

Saint Martin de Porres became a Dominican brother and was considered a miracle worker. He became famous among the people for his skills in healing and his work with marginalized people such as widows, prostitutes, mixed race and indigenous people. He founded hospitals and orphanages.

One of the "little stories" concerns Saint Martin de Porres and the ailing Archbishop Don Feliciano de Vega. The Archbishop specially sought this poor mulatto lay brother's assistance because of Saint Martin's spiritual gift of healing. While residing at the Archbishop's residence, Saint Martin continued his daily practice of cleaning toilets

at the convent. He was asked, "Is it not better to be in the house of the Lord Archbishop than in the toilets of the convent?" Martin replied, "I prefer a little time spent in this work than many days spent in the house of the Lord Archbishop," a reference to Psalm 84:10: "I would rather be a doorkeeper in the house of my God than live in the tents of wickedness." One way that ordinary members of the church challenged the pious elite and the oppressive practices of the church was by telling and retelling "little stories" like this when overt questioning of the leaders was not allowed.

Fanny Lou Hamer: A Contemporary "Little Story"

In August 1962, Fanny Lou Hamer heard the call of Jesus and raised her hand. Fanny attended a voter registration meeting led by James Bevell (Southern Christian Leadership Conference—SCLC) and James Forman (Student Nonviolent Coordinating Committee—SNCC) at Williams Chapel Church in Ruleville, Mississippi. Despite her previous lack of awareness about the civil rights movement, Fanny raised her hand when the call went out for volunteers among the dirt-poor sharecroppers, field hands, and domestics who would go to the courthouse the next day to register to vote.[3]

Fanny was forty-four and worked as a field hand for the Marlowe cotton plantation on the Mississippi Delta. Despite their hard work and resourcefulness, she, her parents, and fourteen brothers and sisters were permanently trapped in these demeaning jobs. Slavery was long over, but the discriminatory practices of the plantation system kept all of them in perpetual debt to the company store.

The black church had prepared Fanny to step out in faith. When blacks were treated like nobodies, the black churches preached a gospel that passionately affirmed their humanity. It also taught hymns of faith. Fanny became known for singing in the face of fear, harassment, arrest, imprisonment, and threats of torture and death.

When Fanny and the other volunteers attempted to register to vote at the county courthouse the next day, they were surrounded by a constant flow of white people wearing cowboy boots, carrying rifles, and accompanied by dogs. Repeatedly black applicants were subjected to an impossible

"literacy test" as part of systematic efforts to deny them voting rights. Fanny passed the test on her third attempt, but, as a result, she and her father lost their jobs on the plantation. Threats of violence caused her to flee, leaving her husband and two adopted children behind.

The following summer, Fanny attended the SCLC's citizenship school in South Carolina with six others from Mississippi. On the way home, they encountered several policeman and highway patrolmen when they attempted to sit at the bus station lunch counter in Winona, Mississippi. During the ensuing altercation, they were arrested and subsequently subjected to torture and beatings in the Winona jail. Though they were near death from the merciless beatings, Fanny sang hymns that transformed the despair of victims into faith that dispersed the power of hate and violence.

One of the "little stories" about Fanny's refusal to hate white people occurred in jail during the days following her brutal beating. She struck up a conversation with the jailer's wife who extended a little compassion by offering the prisoners some cold water. In reply to Fanny's comment that she must be a Christian, the woman said she tried to follow Jesus. "Mrs. Hamer assumed the role of counselor and spiritual gadfly in her response. She told the jailer's wife to get out her Bible and read the verses in Proverbs 26:26 and Acts 17:26." The verses condemned those "whose hatred is covered by deceit" and challenged white churchgoers to recognize all people as part of God's creation. Fanny used her faith to radically subvert the oppressive systems that both whites and blacks inhabited.

Fanny condemned the discriminatory behavior of whites but maintained that returning the hatred would only perpetuate injustice. She believed that the civil rights movement promised freedom for whites as well as blacks and should be open to anyone who showed Christ's concern for others. She admonished everyone around her to look for the good in all people, regardless of color.

Fanny went on to become one of the most tireless and effective civil rights workers. Her spiritual gifts of speaking and singing galvanized, inspired, and unified countless groups of activists. Through the turmoil of those years of struggle, Fanny embodied a practical Christianity and her activities can be understood as works of love. She maintained that social sins would not be overcome by

church attendance alone. "Christianity is being concerned about [others], not building a million-dollar church while people are starving right around the corner. Christ was a revolutionary person, out there where it was happening. That's what God is all about, and that's where I get my strength."

Stewards in Our Time

Spirituality is a current popular buzzword. With all the daily pressures and stresses of work, family, and community life, many people, ranging from poor to wealthy, are hungry for deeper meaning in their lives. An infinite variety of books, tapes, videos, talismans, classes, and religious experiences advertise spiritual insights to the purchaser or participant. Many of these resources merely dip into the superficial or sensational aspects of spirituality. In contrast, the spiritual depth many Christians seek is available through the Holy Spirit at all times, if we are open to God's creative activity in our lives.

In many historic Protestant churches, manifestations of the Spirit such as Paul described in 1 Corinthians 12 may be perceived as foreign, overly emotional, irrational, or threatening. Yet interest and participation in healing services, prayer and praise gatherings, spiritual direction, spiritual life retreats, and the like are increasing.

The potential for misuse *is* possible. In his letter to the Corinthians, Paul chastised believers who used their spiritual gift for self-glorification or who self-righteously maintained that their particular spiritual gift was superior to others. Disputes over spiritual gifts arose within a few months of the Corinthian church's formation. Today we still struggle with similar questions! Nevertheless, the potential for abuse should not prevent us from claiming and celebrating these powerful gifts of the Spirit available to us through God's grace.

Charis means grace. The *charismata* are gifts bestowed as an act of divine grace, God's outpouring of love for us. Spiritual gifts are vocational callings by God to ministry within the body of Christ for the upbuilding of the community. *Charismata* are not necessarily identical with natural abilities or talents for which we might take credit and pride.

Where do you see either misunderstanding or misuse of spiritual gifts in our culture today?

List some gifts that you see in your congregation that are being used for the common good.

The Christian church is a *charismatic* community cutting across all denominational, theological, class, gender, ethnic, political, or other divisions. As boldly stated in 1 Corinthians 12:7, *all* Christians are given a spiritual gift for the common good. Each is a steward of a divine gift (1 Peter 4:10). Gifts of the spirit are at once personal and communal. They are not private possessions for an individual's use and enjoyment.

Spiritual gifts fulfill different functions and purposes. Some spiritual gifts, such as preaching, healing ministries, or speaking in tongues, are most suitable for expression within the church's organizational life and worship. Others may be employed in secular ministries in response to God's call. Examples might include teaching, the healing professions, servant leadership, prophetic witness against social injustice, and service with needy people at society's margins.

In 1 Corinthians 12:4-6, Paul differentiates between gifts, services, and activities of the Spirit. Paul's lists of spiritual gifts in 1 Corinthians 12 are examples of spiritual gifts that are important in the communal life of the church. John Wesley drew a distinction between the "ordinary" gifts of the Spirit such as persuasive speech and knowledge in contrast with "extraordinary" gifts such as healing and speaking in tongues.[4] Others expand the definition of spiritual gifts to include all aspects of our God-given spiritual makeup such as talents, interests, and motivations.

John Wesley distinctively focused on the fruits of the Spirit (the embodiment of responsible grace) as the criteria for authentic spiritual gifts. If we carefully test spiritual gifts according to the fruits they bear then there is less potential for abuse. When the fear of inappropriate use is removed, we can then joyously embrace the spiritual gifts graciously entrusted to us by God. In Isaiah 5, the fruits God anticipated from the vineyard were justice (*mishpat*) and righteousness (*tsedaqah*), the enduring standard for the covenant community of faith. Galatians 5:22-23 identifies the fruits of the Spirit as love, joy, peace, patience, kindness, generosity, faithfulness, gentleness, and self-control. In 1 Corinthians 13, which follows Paul's explanation of spiritual gifts, Paul provides the ultimate test: love. Verse 13 eloquently counsels, "And now faith, hope, and love abide, these three; and the greatest of these is love."

In 1 Corinthians 12, Paul urges Christians to carefully and critically discern and embrace the spiritual gift God lavishes on each of us individually for the good of the whole community.

Opening ourselves more radically to the manifestations of the Spirit holds the promise for personal and communal renewal.

Becoming Stewards: Understanding the World

Imagine God surveying God's vineyard today. What fruits would God discover: justice or bloodshed, righteousness or the cry of the oppressed?

In the Old Testament, God repeatedly instructed the covenant community that part of their agreement included care for the widows, orphans, strangers, and other marginal people in the community. In Psalm 72:1-4, the psalmist prays that those with worldly power to dominate might be just and righteous:

> Give the king your justice, O God,
>   and your righteousness to a king's son.
> May he judge your people with righteousness,
>   and your poor with justice.
> May the mountains yield prosperity for the people,
>   and the hills, in righteousness.
> May he defend the cause of the poor of the people,
>   give deliverance to the needy,
>   and crush the oppressor.

In Isaiah 41:17, the prophet described God's unconditional, passionate commitment to the oppressed: "When the poor and needy seek water, and there is none, and their tongue is parched with thirst, I the Lord will answer them, I the God of Israel will not forsake them."

Paul was greatly disturbed with reports about the lack of charity and elitism of the more affluent Corinthians. Wesley invariably exhorted his followers to help the needy and eradicate the sources of their poverty. He also concluded that worldly prosperity could corrupt the development of a mature faith.

There continue to be great disparities between the prosperous and poor in today's world in spite of God's repeated reminders that as stewards of the covenant we are to particularly care for poor and oppressed people. Some analysts say that the gulf between rich and poor is growing. One-fifth of the world's population, or 1.2 billion people, live on one dollar per day or less, and the income of the top two

Make your own list of spiritual gifts that are especially needed in our world today.

What are some examples of the gulf between rich and poor that you see in your community?

Look at your list of your spiritual gifts from the previous session. What are some ways you would like to use those gifts?

hundred billionaires equals the income of the bottom half of the world's population. As in times past, children and women continue to comprise the majority of the hungry, homeless, poorly educated, underpaid, and lacking medical care—especially if they are from other cultural, national, or ethnic backgrounds.

Living in the World

Every Christian is a steward entrusted with divine spiritual gifts and called to use those gifts faithfully for the upbuilding of the community. What are your unique spiritual gifts? When you complete this study, you may want to consider forming a group in your congregation to explore spiritual gifts. Some resources for doing this are listed at the end of this chapter. A spiritual gifts inventory will help you identify and explore your spiritual gifts and how you might be a faithful steward of those gifts in your own community.

How does your congregation recognize, affirm, and celebrate the gifts of its members? Think not only about the gifts used within the congregation (teaching Sunday school, singing in the choir, etc.) but also gifts that people use on God's behalf in the world. Some people may be using their gifts to work for justice in the political life of the community. Others may volunteer in soup kitchens or food pantries. You may have members in the healing professions who use their gifts on behalf of those in need. Consider preparing a special worship service that recognizes spiritual gifts and areas of service.

Initiate ministries in your congregation based on spiritual gifts. You might begin with ministries of hospitality, healing, and discernment. Talk to people in your region who have experience with these ministries. Who are the people in your congregation and community who model stewardship of their spiritual gifts? They may or may not be people customarily considered church leaders. Visit with them to discover their "little story." What do these stories reveal about people's faith and their gifts of the spirit? How do some of these stories from people at the margins challenge the elite in society and the church? What injustices do they expose? How do they inspire and encourage you to practice the justice and righteousness to which God calls you? Consider inviting people with "little stories" to tell them to your church, Bible study group, or Sunday school class.

These practices require intentional effort and commitment, but they can lead to significant personal and communal transformation as the fruit of their efforts.

1. Craig Dykstra and Dorothy C. Bass, "Times of Yearning, Practices of Faith," *Practicing Our Faith: A Way of Life for a Searching People*, ed. Dorothy C. Bass (San Francisco: Jossey-Bass Publishers, 1997), p. 5.

2. This story comes from Alex Garcia-Rivera, *St. Martin de Porres: The "Little Stories" and the Semiotics of Culture* (Maryknoll N.Y.: Orbis Books, 1995).

3. This story comes from Charles Marsh, *God's Long Summer: Stories of Faith and Civil Rights* (Princeton: Princeton University Press, 1997).

4. Randy L. Maddox, *Responsible Grace: John Wesley's Practical Theology* (Nashville: Abingdon Press, 1994), p. 134.

Suggestions for Further Reading

Ammerman, Nancy Tatom; Jackson W. Carroll; and Carl S. Dudley, ed. *Studying Congregations: A New Handbook*. Nashville: Abingdon Press, 1998.

Bakke, Ray, and Jim Hart. *The Urban Christian: Effective Ministry in Today's Urban World*. Westmont, Ill: InterVarsity Press, 1987.

Bass, Dorothy C., ed. *Practicing Our Faith: A Way of Life for a Searching People*. San Francisco: Jossey-Bass, 1998.

Birch, Bruce C. *Let Justice Roll Down: The Old Testament, Ethics, and Christian Life*. Louisville: Westminster John Knox Press, 1991.

Brueggemann, Walter. *The Covenanted Self: Explorations in Law and Covenant*. Minneapolis: Augsburg Fortress Press, 1999.

Bryant, Charles V. *Rediscovering Our Spiritual Gifts*. Nashville: Upper Room Books, 1991.

Buechner, Frederick. *Wishful Thinking: A Seeker's ABC*. San Francisco: Harper & Row, 1993.

Carle, Robert D., and Louis A. DeCaro, ed. *Signs of Hope in the City: Ministries of Community Renewal*. Valley Forge, Pa.: Judson Press, 1999.

Garcia-Rivera, Alex. *St. Martin De Porres: The "Little Stories" and the Semiotics of Culture*. Faith and Cultures. Maryknoll, N.Y.: Orbis Books, 1995.

Harrelson, Walter J. *The Ten Commandments and Human Rights*. Macon, Ga: Mercer University Press, 1997.

Harris, Edie Genung, and Shirley L. Ramsey, *Sprouts: Nurturing Children Through Covenant Discipleship*. Nashville: Discipleship Resources, 1996.

Jennings, Theodore W., Jr. *Good News to the Poor: John Wesley's Evangelical Economics*. Nashville: Abingdon Press, 1990.

Jung, L. Shannon, and Mary Agria. *Rural Congregational Studies: A Guide for Good Shepherds*. Nashville: Abingdon Press, 1997.

Maddox, Randy. *Responsible Grace: John Wesley's Practical Theology*. Nashville: Abingdon Press, 1994.

Marsh, Charles. *God's Long Summer: Stories of Faith and Civil Rights.* Princeton: Princeton University Press, 1997.

Rasmussen, Larry L. *Moral Fragments and Moral Community: A Proposal for Church in Society.* Minneapolis: Augsburg Fortress Press, 1993.

Russell, Letty M. *Church in the Round: Feminist Interpretation of the Church.* Louisville: Westminster John Knox Press, 1993.

Trumbauer, Jean Morris. *Created and Called: Discovering Our Gifts for Abundant Living.* Minneapolis: Augsburg Fortress Press, 1998.

———. *Sharing the Ministry: A Practical Guide for Transforming Volunteers into Ministers.* Minneapolis: Augsburg Fortress Press, 1995.

Vallet, Ronald E. *Congregations at the Crossroads: Remembering to Be Households of God.* Faith's Horizons. Grand Rapids: Eerdmans, 1998.

Watson, Gayle. *Guide for Covenant Discipleship Groups.* Nashville: Discipleship Resources, 2000.

Willard, Dallas. *The Divine Conspiracy: Rediscovering Our Hidden Life in God.* San Francisco: Harper & Row, 1998.

Wuthnow, Robert. *The Crisis in the Churches: Spiritual Malaise, Fiscal Woe.* London: Oxford University Press, 1997.

Stewards of the Good News of Personal Communities I

Rebecca Laird

Read Exodus 16:1-21
John 6:1-14, 25-35

God's gift of community comes to us in many shapes and sizes. The most intimate of those are the personal communities in which we live—our families, our friends, those who are part of our daily lives. Sometimes these are the places where it is most difficult to be good stewards. These are the people whose love and care we often take for granted. And sometimes it is difficult to reach out to others and easy to remain insulated in our personal world. This week and next we will think about what it means to live as faithful disciples of Jesus Christ with those who are closest to us.

● ● ●

Ask any group of people with full stomachs its top priorities and eating and drinking probably won't make the top-ten list. But then ask them again after a day or two of strenuous exercise and little food. Watch how much energy and time are spent on gobbling lunch, gulping down a beverage, and making dinner plans. Most of us eat without thought, drive to the take-out window on a whim, and crawl into our beds unaware of the luxury it is to sleep warm and safe. In any other century, and, indeed in many households and countries today, three square meals a day and a room of one's own remain distant fantasies.

As stewards of all of God's gifts, the very food we eat, the houses that shelter us, and the vehicles that transport us all become tools in our hands to bring blessing to those with whom we share our daily lives. They also remind us that all good gifts, from daily bread to practical wisdom, come from God and are given not for us alone but for the whole company of God's people.

Stewards in Biblical Times

Exodus 16:1-21 tells about forgetfulness, anxiety, insecurity, and greed. How quickly the early Israelites questioned God's

As you read this Scripture passage, note the places you see similar responses from people today.

goodness. Weeks before they had witnessed God's miraculous parting of the Red Sea. And, as the passage begins, they were just days away from their second campsite. They had just left a lovely stopping place called Elim that was reported to have twelve springs and seventy palm trees. But this well-watered shady oasis was not their future home. God's promised land awaited them in Canaan, many arid miles and years away. To get there the Israelites had to step into the unknown, once again walking in faith. Displaced and unsure of the journey, they began to get hungry and thirsty and tired. Their stores of figs and dates, lentils, and cucumbers would have been dwindling. As people on the move, they had no opportunity to grow new crops. They had missed a few meals, but more than that, they knew that each step farther from Egypt would leave them hungry. Things were likely to get worse before they got better. Hungry and fear-filled, they began to complain en masse against Moses and Aaron. They said it would be better to eat and be enslaved than die hungry but free in what they feared was a "God-forsaken" wilderness. Displaced and worried about their dwindling supplies and gnawing stomachs, the Israelites began to think back to Egypt as a place where they at least had food. Their immediate desires for food and security overrode their hopes for long-term freedom.

Once again, in a place where it seemed there were no resources, God surprised the disbelieving Israelites with a display of glory. God's *shekinah*—the shining witness of God's nearness—was made manifest to remind them that this wilderness, however bleak, was God-filled not God-forsaken. God answered their anxiety with a reminder of presence. Then God got practical and provided food. At night the Israelites got meat; quail descended upon the camp, and the Israelites went to sleep with full stomachs and visions of barley loaves in their heads. When they woke up they looked at the white stuff scattered on the ground and asked "Manna?" which literally means, "What is it?" They were reluctant to eat what they had not seen before. Probably with some measure of exasperation, Moses said, "It is the bread that the Lord has given you to eat" (Exodus 16:15). Then Moses explained God's ground rules: They could eat what they needed but were not to hoard any for the next day. They were to literally eat their "daily bread" and put no thought toward tomorrow's breakfast. This

movable community had to trust in God's constant generosity to provide exactly what they needed as it was needed and not before. Each family group was to take what was needed in equal shares; no one was permitted to get rich or fat on manna. Indeed, those who secretly took extra found their excess rotted overnight, as perishable foodstuffs would in a tropical climate.

The Israelites had left Egypt willingly but were not yet fully aware that their new life of faith would be based on a whole new way of living. There would be food, but it wasn't bread like they used to eat in Egypt. Still it was food, and it was enough. In fact the bread they had in Egypt, however tasty, was the result of their backbreaking labor. In the wilderness, God's daily bread is a gift of divine hospitality given to those utterly dependent on God's goodness.

In the New Testament in John 6, Jesus finds himself surrounded by another hungry crowd. This time the disbelievers were his disciples who worried not so much about bread but about money. How would they find the money to feed all these people? Jesus didn't let a lack of money stand in the way of caring for people. He took what one boy freely gave and turned it into enough. This miracle, the only one that is retold in all the Gospels, explains God's economy—God gives resources to us in order to get them through us, and only God knows the good our gifts can do. When we place our meager gifts in the hands of God's sent and chosen one, a little becomes enough to provide for many. A few verses later, some of those who have been divinely fed ask Jesus a probing question: "Why did you come here?" Jesus answers with a two-layered answer. He has come to point back to the God that rained down bread from heaven to quench physical hunger for the Israelites and also to point forward to the same God who provides spiritual bread—the "staff" of life—that gives us the energy to walk with faith and to extend hospitality. The bread of heaven will eternally feed our hearts and never leave us hungry or thirsty again.

Where have you seen some miracles of hospitality?

Stewards in History

By definition hospitality requires an invitation and an open door: people who are not yet well known are welcomed inside the safe and personal space of another and offered food, drink, safety, and kindness. The word "host" or

Who would the members of your congregation say are the "strangers" in your community?

"hostess" originally meant "a lover of strangers." Extending care to others was understood as a part of the *hesed*, the self-giving love that God extended toward Israel and that they were to extend to one another. This generous reciprocity was a part of the covenant God initiated with the Israelites when God promised to be their God and they vowed to live as God's chosen people.

Ancient Israelites were a community-oriented people who abided by a code of hospitality. Travelers were to wait in an open space as they neared an encampment or village. Those who lived there were to approach before nightfall to offer an invitation. Often strangers were screened outside the village wall. A traveling teacher might be asked to give a talk. Others traveling on business might produce a letter of recommendation from a prominent merchant or government official or other document to describe their reason for travel. When all were introduced and satisfied of benign intent, strangers were brought inside, their feet washed, and they were offered the best the host possessed. Most visitors stayed no more than a night or two as to not disrupt the household. These guests, in temporary need, received welcome and nourishment and set off again with provision for the next leg of the journey. The community also abided by levitical laws that protected sojourners and aliens from destitution and harm. Crops on the borders of fields were to be left for the poor and traveling to harvest. Employers couldn't exploit foreign workers, and all were to receive a sabbath rest. Fugitives fleeing persecution were to be fed and sheltered from unjust treatment.

What are some ways you or your congregation provide hospitality to strangers?

Jesus pushed the priority of hospitality one notch higher when he declared in Matthew 25 that whosoever cared for "the least of these" welcomed Jesus directly into their midst. In the twentieth century, Dorothy Day, one of the founders of the Catholic Worker movement, radically devoted herself to welcoming Jesus in every poor soul she encountered in New York City's streets. Likewise, Mother Teresa of Calcutta often said that the destitute poor she helped, however smelly or dirty, were actually Christ in the distressing disguise of the poor. Jesus' radically inclusive commands reconstituted the household, expanding it from a biological or economic unit to a spiritual one meant to include those of differing status and backgrounds. Jews and Gentiles, male and female, slave and free were called into community to worship together and extend the hand of

fellowship and offer the table of welcome to include all who believed.

From the earliest days of the Christian church, Christians were to deliberately extend a welcome and collect an assortment of unlikely people around the table of fellowship. Hospitality, contrary to our contemporary notion of putting out the china and serving our finest fare for those we would like to impress or invite into our churches, was, in earlier centuries, a fundamental human activity of offering food, shelter, protection, and provision to strangers. The best was to be offered to those we may never see again, may never benefit from, may never count among our church membership. Recall how Jesus told the parable of the great dinner. Those invited found excuses not to come and the master instructed his steward to go out and compel the poor, the crippled, the lame, and the blind to come in (Luke 14:16-24). In Jesus' view, to take care of those who had few needs was hardly hospitality. Hospitality was an act that recognized the humanity of all who travel life's way—we all need to eat, to sleep, and be safe while we do. We all need a kind word and a welcome when far from home and weary from a long day. In the book of Revelation, we, the church, are pictured as a host with Jesus knocking and asking to come in. Thus, acceptance of Christ through faith is understood as an act of spiritual hospitality (Revelation 3:20).

By the fourth century when Emperor Constantine made Christianity the official religion of the Roman Empire, hospitality began to reach beyond the local home and faith community. Hospitals and hostels were created to care for the poor, the orphaned, the widowed, and the sick. At his death, Basil, Bishop of Caesarea, was eulogized for the institutions and hospital he initiated as public response to a severe famine. Little by little, hospitality began to move out of the home as strangers and those in need were cared for anonymously and at a distance. Also during the fourth century, monasteries began to offer shelter and food for pilgrims, those who began to travel for religious reasons, seeking to retrace the steps of Christ or to set themselves apart from society for holy purposes. Benedict, who lived for parts of the fifth and sixth centuries, wrote a "rule" or way of life for his monks that emphasized the centrality of receiving every guest as Christ in a personal encounter.

Do you think providing hospitality to strangers is more or less difficult today than in earlier times? In what ways?

What benefits have we lost by having institutions rather than individuals provide hospitality?

What might we do to regain some of those benefits in our own lives?

During the Middle Ages, those in need turned mostly to monasteries and church-run hostels and hospitals. By the sixteenth century many of the hospitals became municipal institutions. While necessary care was still available, the key components of Christian hospitality that offered personal relationship while providing necessary sustenance became severed. Those that received a personal welcome were usually those who had status or whose welcome held promise of some benefit. Hospitality had become a public benefit rather than a Christian spiritual practice.

When the Protestant Reformation rocked the church in the sixteenth century, scathing critiques of personal extravagance and discrimination in the recipients of one's personal hospitality resounded. John Calvin declared that welcoming those fleeing religious persecution was a most "sacred" kind of hospitality. Both Calvin and Martin Luther advocated frugality and simplicity of life and saw this most often lived out in domestic life, where people in need would reach out to family and friends. No longer was there a clear emphasis on extending oneself to other classes, races, or status in society.

In the eighteenth century, John Wesley, by encouraging people to meet in homes for building relationships and nurturing new believers, reinvigorated the link between church and home. He reinstituted community love feasts, modeled after the *agape* (self-giving love) table fellowship of the early church. Love feasts offered simple food, often just bread and water, and were based on an open-door policy. All who requested a ticket could attend. Wesley advocated regular face-to-face encounters between people of all kinds. He encouraged his followers to visit the poor and sick in their homes. When asked why it was important to feed unbelievers Wesley replied, "Whether they will finally be lost or be saved, you are expressly commanded to feed the hungry, and clothe the naked. If you can, and do not, whatever becomes of them, you shall go away to everlasting fire."[1] Additionally, the creation of shared homes for widows and local efforts to care for the sick poor reclaimed some of the benevolent, class-transforming impulses found in the early church.

In the nineteenth century, as the United States began to move west and waves of new immigrants landed in the urban areas, relief efforts and missions to aid the masses picked up the thread of hospitality. Early Sunday schools

were established to teach the young, before public schools and libraries. By the late nineteenth century, activities that were once household activities—growing food, providing education, sewing, caring for the sick and elderly—began to be accomplished by specialized institutions and industries. By the twentieth century, extended families no longer lived in proximity, and families were smaller. People left home to work rather than staying home to work the farm. Home became a place of personal refuge to retreat from the world of work and stress rather than a place where someone was always home and a little was in the larder to be shared. Today, all too often, home is where no one is found for hours on end each day. When tired, sick, lonely, or in need of care, no one is home.

Stewards in Our Time

In our culture, one of the clear mottoes is "more is better." Being happy with enough food for each day or even wrestling to define the fine line between "enough" and "more" can easily be misinterpreted as a lack of ambition or setting minimal goals in our success-oriented society. Acts of hospitality, unless they seek to help us get ahead or noticed by someone influential, are deemed time-wasters or acts offered to gain advantage or perks. Likewise, our credit-oriented system of commerce distances us from the first-hand evidence of God's involvement in providing what we need. We go to supermarkets and buy bread that looks nothing like the wheat from which it was made. Meat comes wrapped in plastic, distancing us from any reminders that an animal's life was sacrificed for us to eat and live. Great warehouses allow us to fill our freezers with food for a month, leaving little need to pray for daily bread. Water pours forth from taps in our kitchens, and the pipes that carry it from distant lakes are hidden from view. Our houses with their locked doors insulate us from other's needs. Some can honestly say they know neither strangers nor those in need—they simply aren't encountered in a life where one moves from a fenced-in house into a locked car before entering a secure office building. Underlying all of these symptoms is one great cultural belief—God helps those who help themselves, so God must especially like the self-sufficient, the ambitious, and the able.

As Christians, our faith calls us to counter these cultural

What are some ways to practice hospitality in a society where no one is at home on most days?

To what extent do you feel pressure to be consistently self-sufficient, ambitious, and able to handle the tasks and problems that come your way?

If you were to "have faith for my daily bread and take only what I need so that others may also eat," what would you do differently?

In what ways would you like to act as a conduit of God's goodness to others?

pulls that idealize individualism and material success. We are admonished to pray for "daily bread" and regularly give thanks for the rain, the soil, the sun, the seeds, the creatures, and the many human hands that collectively provide us with what we need. We are to gather and use what we need without hoarding for the future. We are to welcome strangers, bidding them to feel at home with us, not so they will feel compelled to join our group, but because they need to eat and to belong with other people. And we are challenged by the mysterious truth that God provides us both baked bread and spiritual bread as a gracious gift, not as pay for work well done, but as a response of love and care. As recipients of these freely given gifts, we respond by doing likewise to those with whom we share our lives.

Becoming Stewards: Understanding the World

In modern parlance, the "hospitality industry" exists to run hotels and provide for people when they travel. No one with resources needs to knock on the door to anyone's private home to stay alive on a journey as ancient people did. Today, if God were to rain down bread on hungry communities, we would call the Environmental Protection Agency and request a chemical analysis before swallowing one bite.

The challenge of faith brings us face-to-face with the issues of forgetfulness, anxiety, insecurity, and greed faced by the Israelites long ago. While society and economic systems have drastically changed, the human tendency to forget God's past gracious acts and let anxieties about the future dictate our attitudes and actions have not. We still fall prey to grumbling and anxiety when facing uncertainties about the future. These passages of Scripture are not telling us to stand outside in the morning waiting for breakfast to fall from the heavens. Instead they address the core stance of our hearts. Do we trust that God will provide, even if what God provides differs from our expectations? Do we understand that we are conduits of God's goodness to others? Do we let our fears of the future keep us from generously giving of our current resources and time? These perennial questions help us begin to understand how we are to live as gracious recipients of God's bounty and responsive hosts to others in God's global family.

Living in the World

A hospitable life begins with cultivating a hospitable heart. Can you make room for the concerns and cares of others? The first act of a hospitable heart is to recall the times and ways each of us has received freely from another's hand. What acts or attitudes made us feel at home in another's presence?

Once you've identified the characteristics that create an atmosphere of welcome, survey your home. Does it say welcome? The story has been told of a professor who piled his books on every chair in his home. When people came to visit, he sat in the one empty chair oblivious to the awkwardness of others. No one stayed long. They soon tired of standing and looking down at the professor but were unsure if they could clear a chair and settle in. To be welcoming, a home doesn't need to be perfect (in fact, most people feel more welcomed in a home that looks lived in) but prepared for guests. If people know there is a place set for them, a hook to hold their hat and coat, and a story that will be told over dinner, they will feel welcome.

For the church community, similar questions need to be addressed. Is the church accessible? Can people enter in the building if they are in wheelchairs or unable to walk up stairs? These are not just legal issues; they are hospitality issues. Do you clearly invite people in and help them know where to sit, what to expect, where they will find parking spaces, classrooms, restrooms, hymnbooks—anything that will allow them to be at ease? Do you actively invite newcomers into situations where they get to know others personally and not just formally? Listen to your language. Are you communicating in a way that anyone can join in, or are you using religious language or telling stories that only the initiated or long-term members will understand? To a first-time guest, this feels like being the only Spanish-speaking person in a roomful of Swedes—it doesn't feel like home.

Finally, commit yourself to deliberate action. Hospitality is rarely random. It takes initiative and planning. Individuals must take initiative and ask others who they are and whether they would like to share some food, drink, or conversation. Shared hospitality often provides a structure for welcoming others in. A network of people may host a person visiting from another country for an extended time so that no one is

List some characteristics of your home that create an atmosphere of welcome.

What acts of hospitality might you do personally for people who come to your church?

What acts of hospitality might your church do?

unduly stretched. A coalition of churches may offer hospitality to the homeless. Several single people may jointly host a monthly dinner party with each bringing a dish to share to ease the work of offering welcome. Whatever the specific act, at its heart hospitality happens when one who has been fed and cared for freely opens up one's life to another.

1. John Wesley, *The Works of John Wesley*, vol. 1: Sermons I, 1-33 (Nashville: Abingdon Press, 1984), pp. 545-46.

Stewards of the Good News of Personal Communities II

Rebecca Laird

Each of our lives, for better or worse, is bound and shaped by our relationships. The quality and purpose of the relationships we have with others is a core concern of the Christian community. The very word "community" is a multifaceted word we use to describe the connection we have through common purpose, geographical proximity, shared vision, and like-minded mission or interests. Henri Nouwen, the author of many books on the spiritual life, has said, "Community is a mosaic in which every person is a little piece of a different color that when seen together show us the face of God." Who wouldn't want to be a part of this beautiful unity called community? But scratch a little deeper, and we all must admit that our experiences of community are not all harmonious. Community has another side. According to Nouwen, "In every community—whether family or congregation—there is always someone who for someone else is a hair shirt, but that is essential for authentic community."[1] Community isn't a sentimental, loving group that never disagrees. If it were, none of us real and sometimes grumpy people would have a place in it. Instead, community is the place where people of faith struggle to live together, love and serve each other, and follow God's call to mission and care in the everyday world.

Stewards in Biblical Times

The wandering Israelites understood themselves as a community united by a shared legacy of suffering and liberation. Side by side they had born the terrible burden of slavery and had witnessed the parting of the Red Sea when Pharaoh's armies pursued them. They had learned to rely on faith for the daily supply of manna when they were fearful, hungry, and unable to fend for themselves in the wilderness. And despite seeing firsthand the ways God repeatedly showered them with divine presence and provision, they still found it hard to get along. After all, they were not only a faith

Read Deuteronomy 5:6-21 1 John 4:7-12, 18-21

Name some of your best—and worst— experiences of community.

List some other behaviors that help support community.

community, they were an extended family on the move carrying all of their possessions as well as their emotional baggage from place to place. Early in their years of wandering, God gave Moses the Ten Commandments to teach the Israelites how to live in community with God and each other. In Deuteronomy 5:6-21, Moses, now an old man, gathers the community together forty years later and repeats the Ten Commandments to the next generation. Moses reminds them that they will soon step into and inherit the long yearned-for promised land. Moses wants them to recall that the covenant or binding relationship God initiated with the Israelites at Mount Horeb (called Mount Sinai in Exodus) is not some ancient pact made between God and their grandparents. The commandments are a living agreement that will clarify their responsibilities and allow them to freely live out their lives as inheritors of God's blessing.

The Ten Commandments are often understood as a list of laws that govern personal behavior by waving a big no in front of personal sins like swearing, having fun on the sabbath, having sex (or thoughts of sex) with other people's spouses, or taking things we want but can't afford. Yet these commandments were not understood primarily as repressive rules by the early Israelites. They were a nomadic, tribal people who needed to move beyond clannish identity in order to become a new nation. These commandments were a declaration of community that outlined what would provide for the inner stability of their new society. The commandments summarized the basic demands placed upon the separate clans and tribes so that they might live rightly in God's sight. The commandments are shorthand, indeed as memorable as counting one's fingers, that remind us how family and community obligations and religious commitments are intertwined.

In our time, we often separate the public from the private and the religious from the secular aspects of life. We protest when a municipal law seems to infringe on our family or church decisions—how dare the government tell us how to raise our children! But for the early Israelites, all areas of life were subject to rules of faith. The Ten Commandments were the code of ethics that each one was to know, abide by, and carry in their hearts to restrain abuse and cultivate respect for the shared life of the whole community of God. If all abided by these rules, peace would

be possible in all of the tents. If they disregarded these rules, tension, anger, and violence would erupt amidst a people who knew each other's business and depended upon each other in times of crises. By keeping God's commands their energies would not be dissipated by infighting and jealousies. Instead, they would be a community ready to step into God's good future.

As a pragmatic teaching tool, the Ten Commandments outline a way of life that respects the needs of all concerned:

1. The God of Israel has proved faithful and deserves priority. Remember where your power comes from and where your loyalty belongs.

2. The God of Israel is a living God who can't be captured in wood or stone. So don't try to create God in your own image and certainly don't pass down these limited pictures of God to future generations like musty heirlooms set in stone. The God of Moses is the great "I AM," who exists beyond time and space and is knowable but cannot be owned or freely interchanged with other gods.

3. God's name, YHWH, means "I AM WHO I AM" or "I WILL BE WHO I WILL BE." God's name reflects the majestic ever-living, ever-present qualities of God. To demean God's name shows disrespect to the person of God. In ancient cultures to be told someone's name was to be given the key to understanding who they were, the people to which they belonged, and the special qualities they possessed. To demean a name was a verbal blow to one you claim to love.

4. Time is a gift that is to be measured by a sacred timepiece held in God's hands. To cease work, stop pushing, limit strenuous activity, and slow down to savor the life you are given, the people you live with, and the God who made you will lead to your lasting well-being. The God of creation made a whole world and then rested, and so should God's people.

5. All of us age. When it is your generation's time to lead, don't exclude the elders, your parents, from the household or from their rightful roles as teachers even when they no longer are productive. However imperfect

---

For each commandment, list some of the ways we fail to keep these commandments in our time and the way it affects our life together.

1.

2.

3.

4.

5.

they are, they gave you breath and nurtured you. And one day you will be old. Treat them as you want to someday be treated. Respect them as the carriers of the tradition you and your children will inherit. (In a poverty-stricken community, setting aside those who didn't contribute to the hard labor necessary to stay alive would have been a temptation.)

6.

6. Everyone knows killing is bad and has prohibitions against it. This commandment is not outlining a new idea but rather posting a reminder that violent, purposeless slaughter and vengeance killing makes community life impossible. In an interconnected community, disregarding the sacred nature of life severs civil relationships. These people lived closely connected lives. To kill a member of any of the extended clans was to create an atmosphere of hatred that could consume the fledgling nation of Israel.

7.

7. In ancient Israel, the sexual relationship was not a matter to be negotiated between consenting adults. It was an issue that had an impact on the whole community. If a married woman with no economic resources of her own had sexual relations with another man, whose children would she bear? Whose economic responsibility would they or she be? Whose tent would she return to at night? And if in God's sight marriage is a sacred arrangement, whose trust is violated? His? Hers? The children's? Her parents'? God's? The answer to this multiple-choice quiz in ancient Israel would have been— all of the above. Adultery was a crime against the whole extended family.

8.

8. Taking the possession of another violates his or her sense of safety and security. It also robs the thief of self-respect, and if left unchecked, stealing, like any repeated wrong, can erode one's moral conscience.

9.

9. To give false testimony is to lie about another person. A person of goodwill and fine character can be ruined and become the subject of suspicion by unfounded accusations. Truth and trust allow a society to flourish. Frivolous, insincere talk peppered with downright lies puts untrue ideas in the minds of those who otherwise

would treat another with respect and love. Slander makes people look over their shoulders with fear of being misunderstood or misjudged.

10. When we look over the fence to our neighbor's house and want what we glimpse inside—whether the goods, the spouse, the happiness, or the success—we are blinded to God's generosity toward us. Instead of rejoicing in our own good fortune to be alive, we begin to downgrade our lives as they are mirrored back in comparison. This vigorous desiring makes us petty and circumvents the joy known by those who value their own lives and are free to rejoice in other's blessings.

10.

When we read these commandments as practical rules that allow for positive relationships rather than as a list of prohibitive behaviors, we can see anew how personal ethics have an impact on the health of the whole community.

First John emphasizes the importance of ethical behavior and right belief within a New Testament faith community. The original community of believers that received this letter had split. A group had left, and the author of the epistle is eloquently asking, How can you say you love God whom you can't see but hate those closest to you? Perhaps those that left felt that as long as they were personally close to God their treatment of others didn't matter. Maybe they felt that they only had to love those in the community who agreed with their interpretation of the faith. Scholars debate why a group had left but agree that the letter is written to a small church community that was having problems loving one another. To this divided church, the author of the epistles reminds us of the hard truth: "Those who say, 'I love God,' and hate their brothers or sisters, are liars; for those who do not love a brother or sister whom they have seen, cannot love God whom they have not seen" (1 John 4:20). We not only have to love those who agree with our interpretation of things, we must also love all whom God loves, for they too are "born of God" (4:7) and thus spiritual kin.

Stewards in History

The Bible shows us how God's love and commandments were lived out in greatly varied social settings. The ways that those who followed God understood themselves and their

What do you think God requires of us as members of a family or civic community?

communities had an impact on their understanding of who belonged to God and what was required of them as God's people.

The Tribal Community

The early Israelites were a tribal group organized by informal but mutually understood kinship ties. Territorial groups of clans banded together in tribes for mutual protection and help. These tribes understood themselves as one part of the whole people of Israel. Tradition refers to the twelve tribes of Israel with each tribe arising from the sons of the patriarch Jacob. Biblical lists throughout the Bible, however, differ on the number and names of the tribes. The important aspect of the tribal unity remains: they knew themselves to be bound together by a common ancestor, shared history, and a promised future.

The Nation Kingdom

Sometime near the first millennium B.C., Israel formed a nation/state with a monarchy. During this period, Israel began to understand itself as a nation linked to a particular area of land. Kings were crowned, and after a brief period of unity, the nation split into the Northern and Southern Kingdoms of Judah and Israel. Under King Solomon the Temple was built to give a permanent home to the religious and ritual life of Israel. In the sixth century B.C., the Babylonians overran Judah and destroyed the Temple, sending the Israelites into exile. From this time onward Israel clung to its ritual life to preserve its identity while its people were scattered.

The Early Church

In what ways is your congregation similar to or different from these early churches?

By the time of Jesus, the Jewish people remained scattered. Under Roman rule, synagogues existed and the Jews were free to gather for worship. After the return of Jesus from the dead, his early followers met in homes for worship and meals. The *ekklesia*, the Greek term for the church, literally meant the assembly or group that met in someone's home. Entire households (*oikos*, in Greek), which included immediate relatives, extended family, slaves, hired workers, tenants, and sometimes those who practiced a similar vocation or trade, joined in the new community of faith. Welcome was also extended to widows and orphans. When the New Testament letters refer to the "house of

Stephanas" or "Chloe's people" the reference is to both those who worship in a particular home and to those who are part of the daily workings of that household. The early church understood that within its membership, there would be those who came into the household of faith by choice, others by birth or because of extended family relationships. While no one was compelled to believe when the head of the household was converted, most followed and identified themselves with Christ. New converts were regularly added to the house churches. These groups were not closed or uniform. The household of faith included people who were at various levels of commitment and understanding. It included male and female, slave and free, Jew and Greek. Instead of shared ancestry, nationality, or familiar religious practices or rituals as the organizing principles, belief in Jesus Christ brought these people together. Often, they struggled against each other and competing cultural standards and religious views held by others in their pluralistic society. Most of the epistles, like 1 John, were written to the early church, when they found it hard to be faithful to Christ and loving toward each other.

The Monastic Way

Women and men called to a life of prayer and service have joined in a shared community life since the early church. First Timothy refers to an order of widows devoted to prayer. Acts tells us communities met in homes for spiritual enrichment and sharing. In the fourth century Athanasius, Bishop of Alexandria, wrote about the life of Antony, a hermit monk who had gone to the Egyptian desert to pray. Other ammas and abbas, or spiritual mothers and fathers, provided spiritual guidance for those who traveled far to learn from them and to live with them for a while. Around the year 500, Benedict, an Italian monk who had gone out to live a holy solitary life, found himself elected abbot of a nearby monastery. In this early community, like many of our own time, things did not go well. Benedict eventually chased away those monks who had first begged him to lead them after some had tried to poison him. After this experience Benedict wrote *The Rule of St. Benedict*, which describes a practical and contemplative rhythm of Christian communal life. Benedict's rule is based on two ideals. First, we must cultivate our awareness and be mindful of God. Whether we are doing manual work or studying the Scriptures, we are to

What activities in your daily life help you be mindful of God?

In what ways do members of your congregation provide spiritual nurture and support for one another?

What are the most important places of community in your life?

continually recall that all can be prayer when we look and listen for God's presence in everyday life. Second, every encounter with another person is a means for welcoming Christ. Benedict taught his monks to receive every guest as if one were serving Jesus himself. Benedict's second try at community thrived so well that fifteen centuries later, communities around the world still adhere to its time-tested wisdom.

Methodists in England

The eighteenth-century Methodists in England were organized in societies that promoted soundness of heart and life through regular prayer, reflection, and self-discipline and through providing care for others. The societies were divided into classes of about twelve people who were visited weekly by a leader, who became the spiritual overseer and direct contact for these people. Some also voluntarily organized themselves in smaller groups of five to ten people for intensive spiritual nurture and support. These prayer bands provided an accountability system that allowed Christians to ask of each other: How is it with your soul? What known sins have you committed? What are your temptations? These small groups of spiritual care and Christian community galvanized the Methodists and propelled them in transforming their lives and the society in which they lived.

Stewards in Our Time

We live in a time that prizes individuality and mobility. Most people move several times in a lifetime remaking friends at each place and struggling to find a place to belong. Periods of loneliness and social isolation are common. In early centuries many people lived among those who shared a common heritage, language, and religious allegiance. We don't. Diversity and plurality increasingly describe our society. These social realities make us long for a lasting sense of community but make it difficult to create.

According to Jean Vanier, founder of the L'Arche communities where the mentally disabled and mentally abled live together for the purpose of "being with" rather than "doing for" each other, vibrant communities combine a goal with a sense of belonging. In other words, communities exist for a purpose beyond their own needs for friendship and support. The early church was consumed with a sense of

being God's instrument in the world. Those that came together around faith in Jesus were from different races, classes, genders, and religious backgrounds. They were a mixed lot of people who struggled to live out the shared life they had been given through the spiritual and ethical teachings of Jesus. Today our understanding of church often centers on a building or a group of people that meets weekly or less often for worship where we may stand and sing together but do not intimately know one another. For many people their most significant relationships outside of immediate family are with coworkers, and one's identity is formed more by work or membership in a club or organization where a sense of mission or vision may be found. Family is rarely understood as a group with a mission beyond economic survival and hopes for sending the children through college. Our limited time and understanding of the role of the communal life leaves many of us longing for a deeper sense of connection.

What cultural factors make it difficult for you to form meaningful communities?

Becoming Stewards: Understanding the World

Just as home needs to be more than the place we come to when it storms or when we are weary, church can also be more than the place where we show up on Sundays. For real community or communion to take place, we need to open our spiritual eyes to see those closest to us as agents of God's love for us just as we are God's answer to many of their needs and longings for them.

The challenges to community life are as real for us as they were for the early Israelites. There are behaviors we simply must not engage in for the sake of the relationships we cherish. No one can consistently betray another's trust, steal another's goods, do bodily harm, or disrespect family members and create a harmonious home or community. But refraining from certain actions to make life better for the whole isn't all that we are asked to do. More is offered, and more is required. If we say we love God, we are commanded to show it by our love for one another.

This call to responsibility and love is a little like being given a pair of tricky new eyeglasses to wear. Everywhere we look to find God, we see the face of a family member, a neighbor, a coworker, a member of our church, or our own reflection. The questions we must answer are: Will we recognize the face of God when we see it in human form?

Name some of the challenges to community life that you face.

Will we willingly be a part of God's loving expression in our everyday world? Will we allow ourselves to love and be loved by God through God's wonderful but imperfect people?

Living in the World

The following exercises or practices are to help you identify your current community and reflect on ways you might direct your time and energies to strengthen your community this week.

1.

1. Identify your core community: Draw a small circle, then draw two larger ones around it so that you have three concentric rings. In the first, inner intimate circle, write the initials of the few people you truly trust and with whom you can be yourself whether they live near or far. In the second, support circle, write the initials of those you spend time with regularly and admire. These are people with whom you feel some emotional and spiritual affinity. In the third, outer responsibility circle, write the initials of those for whom you bear direct responsibility. This may include extended family members, close colleagues, immediate neighbors, and those to whom you are reluctantly bound. When you are finished placing initials in the circles ask yourself the following questions:

   ● What does this map of my community reveal about my interpersonal relationships?
   ● Are there people in the outer circles of my life whom I wish were in my inner circle? What must I do to solidify that relationship?
   ● Are there too many people in my circle of responsibility and too few in my support circle?
   ● Who is my "hair shirt," the person in my community whom I find most difficult to love? How might I show love for him or her? What can I learn about God from that person?

2.

2. What "rules" or "social commandments" do you live by? What "rules" would you like to live by? Can you list the organizing principles for your family's life together? One family realized their "rule" was: Get everyone to school or work and to every

extracurricular activity without killing each other. They decided to revamp their rule as follows: We will pray a short prayer together before going out the door each morning. We will eat dinner together once a week and take a walk afterwards. We will worship together on Sundays, and we will serve at the community soup kitchen one Friday night a month. This "rule" transformed their family from a frenzied group without clear goals into a family that regularly lived out its core commitments.

3. Find a way to meet with someone or a small group with whom you can be honest this week. Call at least one of the people you listed in your inner intimate circle and spend time with them. Think of three to six people in your total community whom you might ask to join you in a prayer circle. You don't have to have a rigorous structure but you will need to agree on some basic elements for your group to thrive. You will need to agree to keep what is shared within the group. Then you can settle questions of who will lead, when, where, and how often you will meet. (A trial period of a few weeks is often wise. Then you can assess or restructure as needed. You might then also determine how you will embrace or serve others outside of the group. Most healthy groups exist for more than their own good.) The most important element is to begin meeting and praying. God will be present among you.

3.

1. Henri Nouwen, "Parting Words," *Sacred Journey: The Journal of Fellowship in Prayer*, 46 (December, 1996), p. 13.

Suggestions for Further Reading

Bass, Dorothy C. *Receiving the Day: Christian Practices for Opening the Gift of Time.* Practices of Faith Series. San Francisco: Jossey-Bass, 1999.

Brown, Raymond E. *The Community of the Beloved Disciple.* Paramus, N.J.: Paulist Press, 1979.

Dawn, Marva J. *Keeping the Sabbath Wholly: Ceasing, Resting, Embracing, Feasting.* Grand Rapids: Eerdmans, 1989.

Edwards, Tilden. *Sabbath Time: Understanding and Practice for Contemporary Christians.* Nashville: Upper Room Books, 1992.

Foster, Richard J. *Celebration of Discipline: The Path to Spiritual Growth.* San Francisco: Harper & Row, 1988.

Kalas, J. Ellsworth. *The Ten Commandments from the Back Side.* Nashville: Abingdon Press, 1998.

Kirkpatrick, Thomas G. *Small Groups in the Church: A Handbook for Creating Community.* Bethesda, Md.: The Alban Institute, 1995.

Muller, Wayne. *Sabbath: Remembering the Rhythm of Rest and Delight.* New York: Doubleday, 2000.

Pohl, Christine D. *Making Room: Recovering Hospitality as a Christian Tradition.* Grand Rapids: Eerdmans, 1999.

Postema, Don. *Catch Your Breath: God's Invitation to Sabbath Rest.* Grand Rapids: CRC Publications, 1997.

———. *Space for God: The Study and Practice of Prayer and Spirituality.* Grand Rapids: CRC Publications, 1985.

Shenk, Sara Wenger. *Why Not Celebrate!* Intercourse, Pa.: Good Books, 1989.

Stewart, Columba. *Prayer and Community: The Benedictine Tradition.* Maryknoll, N.Y.: Orbis Books, 1998.

Thompson, Marjorie J. *Family, The Forming Center: A Vision of the Role of Family in Spiritual Formation.* Nashville: Upper Room Books, 1997.

———. *Soul Feast: An Invitation to the Christian Spiritual Life.* Louisville: Westminster John Knox Press, 1995.

Vanier, Jean. *Community and Growth.* Translated by Ann Shearer. Paramus, N.J.: Paulist Press, 1989.

Stewards of the Good News of Economic Communities I

Sondra Ely Wheeler

Of all the issues that affect our lives together as families and congregations, money is one of the most difficult. When we think of stewardship we often think of the money that we give to support the budget of our church. However, if we believe that all we have is a gift from God, then we are called to be faithful stewards not only of the money that we give to the church but also of all our financial resources. This week and next we will think together about how stewards use the money that God has entrusted to our care.

Read Deuteronomy 15:7-11
Acts 2:43-47
Acts 4:32-35

● ● ●

In the sense in which we use the word "economics" today, we might suppose that the Bible doesn't have much to say about it. Certainly the Bible does not discuss budgets or gross national products or rates of growth. Economics as a social science simply did not exist at the time these texts were written. But in another sense, the Bible has a great deal to say about economics if we remember the origin of the word itself, which comes from the Greek words for household (*oikos*) and law (*nomos*). Economics meant the arrangements by which the needs of all members of the household were supplied. In that sense, concern for the shape of economic community is woven throughout the Scriptures. Significantly, the image of the steward comes from this context of the management of a household.

Stewards in Biblical Times

The first reading comes from the central portion of Deuteronomy that occupies chapters 5–26, from the heart of the covenant law handed down through Moses at Sinai. In the passage immediately preceding this (15:1-6), God has instituted the sabbath year, which calls for all debts within Israel to be canceled every seventh year. Lending and borrowing practices

What does this reading have to say to us about the way we handle borrowing and lending in our culture?

were very significant within the social and material system of ancient Israel. When illness or bad weather or some other problem reduced the harvest, both the food supply and the seed for the next year were also reduced. Borrowing was the only way that Israel's poorest inhabitants could get by. And so Jewish law required lending without interest and the forgiveness of debts every seventh year. Their primary purpose for these laws was to enable the poor to participate in and contribute to the community's life.

In that context, the present passage warns against being mean-spirited and refusing to lend what is needed because of the coming cancellation of debts. A grudging and self-serving attitude toward those in need turns neighbors into strangers and competitors and undermines the blessing God intends to give to faithful people in the land they are entering. The language used in the passage about the needy "crying out to the Lord" recalls the story in Exodus, when God hears the people who cry out under the oppression of Egypt. Just as Egypt made itself into an enemy of God by its hard-heartedness, so might God's own people incur judgment if they are indifferent to their most vulnerable fellows or willing to profit from the misfortune of others.

What does this picture of the early church have to say to us and our congregations today?

The readings from Acts give us a positive model that is a contrast to the "tight-fistedness" that holds on to what one owns in the face of others' need. They tell us about the infant Christian community that is gathered immediately after the day of Pentecost and the inspired preaching of the apostle Peter. These converts are newly baptized and rejoicing in the mercy and goodness of God. They spend much of their days together, given over to the joy of worship and teaching and shared meals. They are overwhelmed with the fullness of God's blessing, and it is natural for them to respond with generosity. They are experiencing abundance and the delight of being part of this new fellowship, and so they are free of all anxious self-protection and all need to defend and identify themselves by what is theirs. Possessions could be held in common and sold as any had need because the believers shared a deep and sustaining confidence in the overflowing greatness of God's power and grace. It is glad hearts that are truly generous. Here it is no longer a question of lending or even of giving to the needy. Instead, no one claims anything as their own, but rather all share in the goods of all, and the

text tells us, "there was not a needy person among them" (Acts 4:34).

It is worth noting that this observation in Acts echoes the promise of Deuteronomy 15:4-5: "There will, however, be no one in need among you, because the Lord is sure to bless you in the land . . . if only you will obey the Lord your God by diligently observing this entire commandment that I command you today." The commandment in verse 11 to care for the needy who will never cease from the land stands in ironic contrast to this confident promise. It is a testimony to the unfaithfulness of Israel and of the church. The prediction that there will always be poor among us does not give us an excuse for our indifference but calls us to deeper faithfulness.

Stewards in History

In the history of Christian thought and practice, the passages we are considering and the ways of life they represent have gotten a fairly mixed reception. For centuries the church observed the Deuteronomic prohibition against charging interest on loans but applied it only among Christians. The notion of a sabbath year during which debts would be canceled has never been thought binding on the church nor has the church ever embraced it as a regular practice.

Nevertheless, the Christian teaching that calls us to respond to our neighbor's need has had a voice throughout history, even when it is muted by the voices of the culture. A good example is eighteenth-century England in which John Wesley and his followers worked. In those days, industrialization and the concentration of labor in cities were creating lower wages for the working classes. At the same time, the price of basic necessities was going up. This left the poor to choose between stealing what they needed and could not afford or borrowing what they could not repay to provide necessities. Debtors' prisons were a grim reality, where lack of sanitation and the resultant disease often turned into a death sentence.

Wesley's longtime practice of visiting in prisons exposed him to the brutality of conditions there and to the devastation caused to families left behind. Along with providing relief to prisoners and their families and campaigning to remedy the appalling conditions in the jails,

How do borrowing and lending practices in our culture create classes of rich and poor?

Who are the poor in your community, and how are they treated?

How do you think about how much you keep and how much you give away?

Is it difficult to be a faithful disciple of Jesus Christ today if one is rich?

What is the difference between owning your possessions and your possessions owning you?

Wesley used his own money to provide interest-free loans and to establish workers' cooperatives. Part of the dramatic success of the Methodist movement among the poor was in providing alternatives to lethal cycles of poverty, debt, and helplessness.

The communal model of life and property in Acts was not widespread in the early church. Jesus' warnings against wealth and his injunctions about giving away property had more direct influence on the church's understandings of property. Individuals began to practice voluntary poverty. Early church sources such as the Shepherd of Hermas, Origen, and John Chrysostom counseled Christians to be modest if not downright austere in their material lives, and they judged actual wealth to be incompatible with faithfulness. In later years, Clement of Alexandria (c. 200) and others said that it was not wealth but improper attachment to wealth that brought judgment. And so the standard for Christians in dealing with money focused more on generosity and giving to the poor and less on getting rid of private possessions.

When the monastic orders began around the sixth century, their members held all goods in common. In these settings, private and individual ownership was eliminated. All of one's goods were surrendered for distribution to the poor when entering the order. Thereafter, even the food you ate and the clothing you wore belonged to the community. The monasteries provided a setting for those who wanted to follow directly the teaching and example of Jesus in the Gospels. Here they could find freedom from anxiety and self-preoccupation by living in a community where goods were shared. The writings of Christian saints and mystics throughout the centuries tell us clearly about the moral and spiritual power of life in community and the importance of material community if we are to grow in Christian perfection.

After the Reformation, however, Protestants generally rejected the monastic patterns of communal life. Those who wanted to live after the model of the Acts community invented a variety of new structures with varying success and difficulties. These have ranged from the Anabaptist communities of sixteenth century Europe, to the "utopian" Christian communes of the American eighteenth and nineteenth centuries, to the contemporary base communities of Latin America. In the latter, economic

community is part of the foundation for Christian resistance to oppressive social structures. Some of these efforts are impressive and historically significant, but they have been very much the exception and not the rule. They are part of the heritage of Christian faith, and they help to broaden our horizon when we think about our own communities, but they have never been embraced as "normal" or required forms of faithfulness.

Stewards in Our Time

These passages and the forms of community life they reflect are rather remote from the practical experience of most contemporary Christians. Few of us feel a direct and personal obligation to a community beyond our families, and few of use feel an actual duty to supply our neighbors' needs. Certainly we would think twice about lending money if we thought that the debt would be canceled. While we might feel that such a response would be generous and praiseworthy, most Christians would be surprised or even offended if we thought it was a requirement. Even further from our experience and usual way of thinking is the idea that possessions might be held in common: not belonging to any one person but belonging to the community, or even as belonging to God and given by God to meet the needs of all. If these passages have any effect on our lives, it is as an ideal rather than a real expectation of ourselves or one another.

What responsibility do we have for others in our community?

Some of this is because enormous social, cultural, and political changes have occurred since these texts were written. We no longer live as our Hebrew forebears did in clans or tribes, relatively small groups based loosely on kinship. Our economy is no longer based primarily on agriculture and herd animals where social access and participation are the same for all. In the period of Acts (written roughly A.D. 70–90, describing a time forty or fifty years earlier), the urban context and economy are more familiar. There are many languages, nationalities, and cultures. Nevertheless, the place and nature of the church as a community within the larger culture is dramatically different.

What does our culture say to us about these issues?

At this point in Acts, the church is still a clearly distinct minority within the Jewish community. By contrast, nearly two thousand years later we are decisively separated from our Jewish parent tradition. Christians are more plentiful in our modern societies, and it is harder to distinguish Christians from the rest of society. The number of people who believe in God in generally Christian terms is larger than the number who worship regularly. That in turn is larger than the number who would consider their Christian commitment central to their lives and choices. And so the boundaries of the Christian community are considerably less clear.

What influence has your faith had on your decisions about what you do and where you live?

Even among those of us who might claim our faith as central, it is rarely the only or even the most significant shaper of our daily lives. In the standard exchanges between seatmates on airplanes, we ask what someone does for a living, whether they have a family, and whether the trip is for business or pleasure. These are reasonable introductory questions because most modern people order their lives primarily in relation to the work they do to support themselves and their families. Their choices about where to live are related to the demands of their jobs and the well-being of their families. These in turn determine what kind of home or neighborhood they live in, where they worship, and with whom they associate. It is work (and thus economic class) and family status that form the core of most people's identity.

What influence should it have?

Two more observations help to underscore the gulf between our world and the world of the Scriptures. The first is that our work has become more likely to change repeatedly during our lifetime and it often requires relocation even when it remains stable. The second is that what we mean by family has narrowed to include only parents and children, which we see as a portable unit with very few connections to a larger, more extended family or local community. So even the structure of our lives tugs against our embracing this vision of a broader community to which we belong. But that is not all. Our ways of thinking, talking, and judging are shaped by two dominant features of our culture: individualism and consumerism.

Becoming Stewards: Understanding the World

The basic belief system of our society exalts the individual as the center of value and meaning. Each individual must be free to choose and pursue whatever seems good to her or him with the least possible constraint.

This philosophy has contributed to the success of our consumer culture, which emphasizes individual initiative and private reward or penalty. The same philosophy has also encouraged us to accumulate private possessions and personal wealth. At the same time, the consumer culture sends us the same message over and over again: happiness is secured by possessing more and more "things." Our high degree of mobility contributes to the anonymity and transience of our lives, making it easier to look at possessions as our source of identity and well-being. Possessions can be boxed and carted to the next stop; friends, even if one had time to make them, cannot.

And yet we all know that this strategy for seeking human fulfillment does not work. Many people express a sense of frustration with central features of modern life, especially its brutal pace and shallow satisfactions. Nonetheless, it can be very hard and very threatening to withdraw from the role of "consumer" in search of some other, deeper springs of security and joy. One of the ways in which our biblical witnesses serve us is by calling our own culture into question and offering an alternative picture of how we might live our economic lives as the people of God. But economies are by their nature social constructions, part of the task of common life. If the economics of Scripture are to have any impact on our lives, Christians must gather together to consider and evaluate, to challenge and to encourage one another, and to imagine alternative ways of meeting material needs and forming and sustaining communities. Only then can these biblical visions and models help us live more fully and more faithfully.

It is also important to acknowledge the benefits of our economic system as well as its costs. It has shown an unparalleled capacity to generate wealth, and people in the industrialized countries are better off than people have ever been in human history. This affluence has in fact given people an unprecedented range of choices, including opportunities for real growth and fulfillment. In addition, consumer capitalism creates incentives for improvement and innovation, fostering rapid scientific and technical progress which contribute to our welfare immeasurably. Both our individual liberty and our material prosperity are genuine goods, goods in which we as Christians have a special stake grounded firmly in our regard for human beings as embodied and made in God's image.

Does your checkbook reflect the values of the culture or the values of the gospel? Be specific.

What are some alternative ways of meeting your material needs that are suggested by these biblical models?

What are some of the reasons for unequal wealth in your community? What would have to be done to make the distribution of wealth more responsive to human needs and relationships?

List some ways you could share resources with people in your neighborhood.

All that said, however, wealth and the other benefits of capitalism are distributed very unevenly. Globally, growing concentrations of capital seem to hinder the development of democratic institutions and make them less effective where they already exist. In addition, the environmental costs of industrialization in some areas have been catastrophic. It is not clear whether we can reform our existing institutions in such a way that they can help repair the damage and create fair and sustainable alternatives. The world has yet to see a broadscale economy where human needs and relationships retain center stage, where having enough is important, and where fair distribution of goods matters more than maximum output.

If we are to have such a reformation, it will depend on the church offering the world alternatives that value community more than individual autonomy. But dreaming and building such alternatives will take more than technical expertise. We will need nothing less than a conversion of heart, for the Bible's economy of mutual responsibility and shared goods is not based on scarcity but on abundance, not on threat but on security, not on defending against the outsider but on welcoming the stranger. We will need to move from a political economy built on greed to one that is built on our deep need for communion with one another.

Living in the World

Models for economic life that are built on biblical patterns of shared resources and care for one another are not common among contemporary Christians, but they are not entirely absent either. In different locations in the church we find examples of faithful practice in response to the diverse promptings of the Holy Spirit. These range from thoughtful alternatives to our commercialized holidays to sharing major resources like vehicles, machinery, and tools, to actual communal living.

Many congregations have Christmas fairs where members give gifts to Christian missions on one another's behalf and celebrate Christ's birth by caring for his people. What practices are currently a part of your congregation's life? Could you begin planning for alternative ways of celebrating Christmas that involve less consumption? Changing familiar patterns requires support from others, so your group might plan ways to help one another make these changes.

Faithful people who want to reduce their consumption have

formed cooperatives to purchase and share everything from bulk foods to lawn mowers. This practice offers multiple benefits. It brings people together to support each other as they make joint decisions about their economic lives. Together they can think carefully about what their real needs are and how they can use their resources most effectively to meet them. It also makes available new resources to share with others and creates a context for talking together about how that sharing can best happen. Talk with your group about how you decide to make a major purchase. Develop a list of questions that you will ask yourself before you buy.

Groups of committed Christians have found new challenges and new blessings by forming communities where they share living space and resources. Often these communities are organized to serve Christian missions. In communities such as Koinonia Farms and L'Arche, a simple lifestyle and shared resources make it possible for community members to spend their time working for social justice or in direct service to those with special needs. If you have such a community—or a monastery—nearby, you and your group might visit it and talk with the members about the values that support their community. Even though you probably won't move in, some of the values can be incorporated in your everyday life.

In all these efforts, progress is often slow. Real change takes time and involves setbacks as well as successes. In this regard, economic community is like any other kind—it involves hard work as well as sweetness, struggle as well as joy. It is not possible, nor is it necessary, for us to make a sort of spiritual broad jump from our current lifestyle to the community of Acts. We may find the story of Francis of Assisi compelling, but very few of us are free to embrace holy poverty all in a moment! The important thing is that we begin: begin to re-form our ideas and our imagination, our vision of what is possible, and our hopes for what God might do in and through our lives. What matters is that we take steps, however small, in the right direction. Begin by looking at the way you spend your money and deciding on one or two changes you will make this week. And most important of all, remember that the point is not what we are moving away from but what we are moving toward. The aim is not to deprive ourselves of the material goods we now enjoy, but rather to receive the joy that God has for us as we share God's gifts with our brothers and sisters.

What are some realistic ways you might change the way you spend money?

Stewards of the Good News of Economic Communities II

9 Session

Sondra Ely Wheeler

There is always the possibility, and the temptation, of making religion into a comforting place to hide from the griefs and challenges of life in the world. The quiet of the sanctuary, the beauty of the music, the soaring architecture, even the majestic language of liturgy itself, all are meant to awaken us to the presence and reality of God. But they can also serve as just one more distraction. Both the Old and New Testaments return again and again to this danger, that we will focus on the outward forms of devotion rather than its inner core of love and service. It is easy for us to attend more to the acts of worship than to the character of the One whom we worship, the One we are to recognize and to make known among the needy. When that happens, we turn from the life of faith to the mere signs of faith, and when we abandon the actual practices of faithfulness we lose the joy of being the body of Christ and participating in the very life of God in the world. Stewards, by contrast, are to be engaged in the actual care of the household, and their work as stewards is also worship, a kind of proclamation in action of God's goodness and grace.

Read   Isaiah 58:6-10
2 Corinthians
8:1-15

Stewards in Biblical Times

Our passage from Isaiah comes near the end of this long prophetic book, which most scholars believe was written over a period of two hundred years by three different prophets. The different writers share a common task, to bring God's word to the people as they seek to understand all that has happened to them in light of God's power and faithfulness. But the historical situations the prophets have to interpret are quite different from one period to the next, and so are their words of judgment and correction, hope and glory. The writer of Isaiah 56–66 is writing after the fall of both Israel and Judah and after long years of exile. Finally a tiny group returns to the land and begins to rebuild what war and abandonment have left in ruins. Their lot is hard, and despair and disillusionment haunt the community. They wonder, Where is the promised

Where do you think the prophet would see people practicing goodness today?

glory of Israel's vindication? If there is to be any lasting hope for their efforts, it is vital that the people understand the judgment that fell upon them and understand as well God's promise of restoration, peace, and abundance for his people who seek a deep and genuine renewal of Israel's life.

But the prophet wants them to understand that this renewal is not simply a matter of rebuilding the Temple and restoring the rites once practiced there. God had made Israel a people in the first place by rescuing them from the hand of their oppressors and bringing them from slavery to freedom. If they are to be the people rescued by God's mercy and justice, they must also be a people who practice justice and mercy themselves. Imitating God's own goodness in the way they live is not an option for Israel. It is the very heart of her worship and her identity. The people of Israel show that they remember and honor what God has done for them by siding with the oppressed and destitute. They respond to God's mercy and justice toward them by becoming a people of fairness and compassion whose life bears witness to the reality of their God. To this people, not only rescued but shaped by God's grace, the prophet proclaims: "If you offer your food to the hungry and satisfy the needs of the afflicted, then your light shall rise in the darkness and your gloom be like the noonday" (Isaiah 58:10).

What do you think Paul might say to us today?

The text from 2 Corinthians picks up the same theme. The life of the community of faith participates joyfully in the overflowing generosity of God, now seen through the lens of Christ's self-offering for us. A little context will help make it clear. The Macedonian church was itself struggling in a time of economic hardship in the aftermath of war. Because of their own poverty, they might have thought they were exempt from Paul's appeal for help for the impoverished church in Jerusalem. But instead, they implored Paul to let them share in the grace (*charis*) of participating in this offering. This they do out of their own sense of fullness, their gratitude at what God has done for them that overflows into generosity. In delight Paul then writes to the church in Corinth, inviting them to join the Macedonian church in celebrating the extraordinary generosity of God in Christ by responding to the needs of the church in Jerusalem.

Even though Christ is the motive and model for giving,

Paul does not expect the Corinthians to give as Jesus has given. Nor does he expect them to give "beyond their means" as the church in Macedonia has done. Instead, he suggests that the aim of giving among Christians is this: that the abundance of one meets the lack of the other, so that the needs of all may be satisfied, and there may be equality (what Paul calls "a fair balance" in verse 15). He treats the disparities in resources between the churches as a temporary circumstance, which time might easily reverse, and offers them a picture arising from the history of God's liberation of Israel. He reminds them of the terms of God's own "economy," drawing on the story of God providing food to the fleeing slaves in the wilderness. There, each one gathered what manna they could, and no one had either more or less than they needed. Such a picture prizes sufficiency rather than excess, cooperation rather than competition, and equity rather than maximum productivity as the goods of economic life—and it is a far cry from our own definition of economic health.

Stewards in History

The ringing words of the prophets have never entirely been silenced, and the expectation that communities will share with each other continues to influence the church. Even those outside the church acknowledge that these visions of justice and compassion are one of the great moral achievements of Western civilization. But it is easier to praise them than to practice them! Within the history of the church, the degree to which Christians have managed to live out these ideals of mutual care has varied widely. Part of that variation has come about with the changing identity and location of the church within the societies in which it has existed.

Early in Christian history, Christians were a small minority in societies with many varieties of religions. There were Greek and Roman pagan cults, the worship of various deities of Eastern or Egyptian origin, and the small but stubbornly persistent Jewish community. In fact, the church was at first merely a Jewish sect that didn't become visibly separate until the end of the first century. On one hand, this meant that Christian economic practices had little influence on the society as a whole. On the other, it made membership in and loyalty to the church much clearer than it usually is today,

Give some examples of excess in contrast with sufficiency, competition with cooperation, and maximum productivity with equity in the economy of your local community.

What are some "ideals" in our culture that compete with Christian ideals?

Can you identify behaviors of Christians today that are considered foolish by the culture? List them here.

In what ways does Christianity influence our culture today?

where a vague sort of quasi-Christianity influences the whole culture. In the first century, outsiders told of the strange economic behavior of Christians, which they thought was foolish. They spoke of the Christians' practice of welcoming and supporting travelers, of sharing resources with those in need (including outsiders), and even of Christians voluntarily going to share the lot of those condemned to slavery in the mines—a stunning demonstration of solidarity with the oppressed!

In later centuries, the church moved from the edges of society to its center. First Christianity was tolerated and later it was adopted as the official religion of the Empire following Constantine. Inevitably, this had an effect not only on the Empire but also on the church. To some extent, the Christian ideas of justice and sharing were incorporated into the principles of the wider society, at least as ideals. Nevertheless, at the same time the assumptions and practices of the Empire found their way into the church's thought, imagination, and life. The political figure of the Emperor influenced the images of God and of Christ, and the internal organization of the church resembled more and more the ordered ranks of greater and less that characterized the state. The hierarchical pattern of organization and the degrees of rank and privilege that went with it came to be taken for granted, and the prophets' stress on justice for the afflicted and attention to the poor was muted. Certainly Paul's emphasis on equality was replaced by an acceptance of social and material inequality. Through it all, however, continued the thread that made compassion, justice, and equity matters of concern to God and therefore obligatory for God's people.

Efforts to reform the economic practices of the church occurred during the Middle Ages and also the Protestant Reformation. Martin Luther and John Calvin both stressed modestly in lifestyle and almsgiving as marks of Christian faithfulness and sincerity. Later reformers experimented with different degrees of austerity, economic sharing, and commitment to serving the poor in lay communities in sixteenth-century Europe. They found their inspiration in the very texts we are discussing. Many of these models were transplanted to the New World in the nineteenth century. But alongside efforts to reform the church's own practice, throughout Christian history faithful people have

struggled to make the structures of their societies conform more nearly to these ideals of equity, compassion, and generosity. In America, major movements for social reform—including the abolition of slavery, legislation improving working conditions and outlawing child labor, and the push for universal free education—took their impetus from Christian reformers who believed that the words of prophets and apostles could serve as ideals for the nation as a whole.

Stewards in Our Time

In our own century, Martin Luther King, Jr. called the country to account for the denial of fundamental civil rights to many of its citizens, citing the words of Amos from the steps of the Lincoln Memorial. Many of his heirs continue the struggle for racial equality and to make decent housing, adequate food, and medical care available to all Americans. At the same time, organizations like Bread for the World and Habitat for Humanity have used the prophets' calls for justice and the New Testament's calls for equitable sharing within the church to awaken and prick the consciences of believers. These biblical visions of equity and mutual care call us as Christians to participate in public life, recognizing that we are stewards of God's gift of citizenship.

These Scripture passages and others like them are important for the Christian community as we confront the glaring inequities of our fast-developing global economy. We can see the misery and destitution of whole populations who are left behind in the competitive scramble for profit. Of particular concern today is the enormous burden imposed on impoverished countries by international debt. Much of this indebtedness comes from loans that benefited the rulers more than the nations in whose name they were borrowed. In some cases, the projects that the loans were to finance have never been completed. Meanwhile, mandated interest payments alone consume as much as 20 percent of the gross national product in some countries. This is four or five times the spending on health in the same countries where child mortality may approach one in three who die before the age of five.

Both church and secular groups who want to reform this system of international finance and debt structuring have turned to biblical models of equity and participation in

List some of the positive and negative powers of money in our culture and in your personal life.

What are some ways that institutions cause unintentional harm?

economic communities. In fact, the grassroots movement for debt forgiveness for the poorest countries is called the Jubilee campaign, from the year of release in Deuteronomy 15 that we studied in the last session. Even when international lending institutions do not intend to oppress borrowers, they can end up doing so. We must be attentive to the consequences of economic structures as well as their intentions. It does not require malice to do evil. Institutions can themselves be unintentional agents of grave injury. The Scriptures remind us that God is concerned about the human impact of the way we order our political and material lives. God insists that our faith is to be expressed in justice, equality, and compassion, not only at the personal level but also in the way we order our institutions.

Becoming Stewards: Understanding the World

It is a testimony to the power of the biblical tradition and its hold on the conscience of this nation that it has moved so many people to repentance and to a renewed commitment to social justice. Also, it continues to be true in the modern world as it was in many earlier centuries that the church is frequently the only international institution with the resources, the understanding of the local situation, and the moral authority to respond to critical human needs. But it would be misleading to think that we have made steady progress over the centuries.

What contemporary prophets are speaking God's word to us?

There have been brightly lit passages where shared visions of fairness and equity have led to important legislation and major changes in our society as a whole. Christian inspiration and participation helped bring about labor reform, the establishment of the rights of children, the abolition of slavery, and the development of universal public education. There have also been periods when both church and nation have failed to rise to the moral challenge of equity and compassion. Sometimes even those in the church have denied rights, liberty, and opportunity to people and justified it because of supposed differences in breeding or moral quality or even attributed it to the will of God. Most of the time, we can see competing convictions and conflicting judgments within the church as well as outside.

As modern American Christians, most of us benefit greatly from the success of consumer capitalism. The culture

we live in affects us just as the Holy Roman Empire affected Christians in an earlier era. It is not surprising that we are often more comfortable thinking that poverty is the fault of the poor and wealth the reward of the virtuous than we are recognizing that many factors keep the economic playing field from being level. In fact, we must always consider both individual responsibility and the nature of economic systems. As Christians, our biblical heritage makes us sensitive to the moral dimensions of both individual and social life. Justice is required in both our personal actions and our social structures. God calls us to equity and compassion both in our individual economic transactions and in the patterns of distribution in our society. If we take these commitments seriously, we may become more uneasy in our consumer culture and more responsive to the needs of all those we call sisters and brothers.

Living in the World

Like all human beings, Christians are social creatures. We find our vocation and our fulfillment in relation to others. We are both shaping and being shaped by our family, neighborhood, and nation and by their patterns of thought and life. With the advent of mass communication, the shaping force of culture has become more widespread and forceful as ideas and images are instantly transmitted across the miles. In our thriving consumer economy, one of the most powerful forms of popular culture is advertising.

Researchers estimate that the average American is exposed to an astonishing ten thousand advertising messages per day in the form of radio and television commercials, telephone messages, Internet ads, placards, billboards, street signs, and merchandise packaging. We are not consciously aware of all these, but even the images and slogans we overhear or pass by on the street have an effect on our thinking and behavior. Advertising is expensive, with a fifteen-second television ad costing hundreds of thousands of dollars per broadcast, not including the actual costs of design and production. Advertisers pay these costs only because it makes economic sense to do so. In the present highly sophisticated market, no national ad campaign is launched without consumer testing for effectiveness, and only those that generate an increase in profits greater than their total cost ever make it on the air. Commercial messages

In what ways does your faith influence your decisions about what you do and where you live?

How does following Jesus affect your choices about what you eat, what you wear, what you do for a living?

List some ways advertising has affected what you buy.

List some changes you have made or could make in your daily life to reduce the effect of the consumer culture.

persist because, whether we realize it or not, we listen to them and respond by buying the products they promote.

Ours is a society driven and sustained by consumption, by the purchase and use of a mind-boggling array of products, most of which did not exist a few decades ago. Some of these products provide for basic needs: necessary food, clothing, and shelter; basic transportation; and tools we need to do our jobs and care for our families. But many others are created, marketed, and purchased to respond to desires that advertising creates. Sometimes we desire the product itself, such as elegant entrees or extravagant desserts that are shown at their enticing best. Much of the time, however, the desires evoked by the ad are not for the product but are human longing for things the product can't provide: longings for safety and rest, for acceptance and belonging, for excitement and meaning and love. By using carefully crafted images and sounds—like pictures of the perfect family getting into the shiny car in front of the immaculate house with the manicured lawn—the advertisers make us believe that this perfume or cosmetic, fashion or vehicle, alarm system or newest technological innovation will finally give us the happiness and security we have been looking for. Of course, if we put it that baldly the absurdity is apparent, but it is never put baldly. By subtlety and suggestion we are drawn in, and Christians are not immune to the seductions and the false promises of consumer culture. We too are prone to forget that "one's life does not consist in the abundance of possessions" (Luke 12:15).

How do we combat the barrage of messages telling us that we need to buy, to have, and to consume an ever-growing list of things in order to be happy, respected, and fulfilled? How do we resist the constant pressure on us and our children to acquire and spend money on ourselves? Part of the answer is that it will be an ongoing effort, just as the influence and effect of our culture is ongoing and escapable in our lives. If we want to make our earning and spending choices according to biblical values, it will be a constant countercultural exercise. As God's stewards we are called to care for the needs of others and to pay attention to the effects of our choices upon other human beings and upon the earth on which we all depend. This will require thoughtfulness, effort, and discipline. We will need the support of other people who help to remind us of what we believe, what is worth seeking, preserving, and giving our time to.

The effort to live our lives as part of an economic

community that celebrates and testifies to the goodness of God also carries certain dangers. Self-restraint and frugality can turn into anxiety and discomfort over every expenditure and deprive us of the enjoyment of God's good gifts. On the other side, grateful acceptance of God's blessings can gradually shade over into self-deception, as we too readily adapt to whatever kind of lifestyle our culture deems normal and forget the needs of others and our responsibility to them. We need to look carefully at the way we spend and save and give away in order to make our decisions about the work we do, the money we earn, and the things we spend it on in light of what brings the deepest and most lasting joy.

Most of us, asked to conjure up a memory of our greatest satisfaction, will not think of an extravagant dinner or a cruise on a yacht. We may remember the birth of a child, an evening spent in the quiet company of friends, or a time when we were able to speak a word or give a gift that was truly needed. Our ongoing struggle to live lives of economic faithfulness may best be illuminated by remembering that the world is God's gift and that human beings were made to enjoy its goodness together. As God's stewards all that we have been given is a gift from God and we are to care for it on God's behalf. As we trade our time for money and our money for goods for ourselves or others, as we decide how much to keep and how much to give away, we might think about what will give us real joy. To put it most starkly, we can trade the days and hours of our lives for a bank account that will never be enough to make us safe, for clothing and ornaments that will never make us lovely enough to be sure of being loved. Or we can trade it for warmth for someone out on the street on a freezing night, trade it for all the milk a hungry baby can drink, trade it for comfort for those dying in Mother Teresa's slums or those down the road in the local AIDS hospice. To choose the latter is not only to fulfill our obligations to the poor; it is also to share the very life of Jesus Christ in the world, who has come so that his joy might be in us, and our joy might be full.

Calculate how much you give away as a percentage of your income. Is it too much? Too little? Set a goal, and develop a plan to get there.

Suggestions for Further Reading

Clapp, Rodney, ed. *The Consuming Passion: Christianity and the Consumer Culture.* Westmont, Ill: InterVarsity Press, 1998.

Dominguez, Joe, and Vicki Robin. *Your Money or Your Life: Transforming Your Relationship with Money and Achieving Financial Independence.* New York: Penguin Books, 1999.

Durning, Alan. *How Much Is Enough? The Consumer Society and the Future of the Earth.* The Worldwatch Environmental Alert Series. New York: W. W. Norton, 1992.

Foster, Richard. *The Challenge of the Disciplined Life: Christian Reflections on Money, Sex & Power.* San Francisco: Harper & Row.

Luhrs, Janet. *The Simple Living Guide: A Sourcebook for Less Stressful, More Joyful Living.* New York: Broadway Books, 1997.

Mather, Herb. *Becoming a Giving Church.* Nashville: Discipleship Resources, 1985.

Pappas, Anthony, and Douglas A. Walrath, ed. *Money, Motivation, and Mission in the Small Church.* Valley Forge, Pa.: Judson Press, 1989.

Ronsvalle, John, and Sylvia Ronsvalle. *Behind the Stained Glass Windows: Money Dynamics in the Church.* Grand Rapids: Baker Books, 1996.

Sider, Ronald J. *Just Generosity: A New Vision for Overcoming Poverty in America.* Grand Rapids: Baker Books, 1999.

———. *Rich Christians in an Age of Hunger: Moving from Affluence to Generosity.* Nashville: Word Publishing, 1997.

Schut, Michael, ed. *Simpler Living, Compassionate Life: A Christian Perspective.* Harrisburg, Pa.: Morehouse Publishing, 1999.

Vallet, Ronald E. *Stepping Stones of the Steward: A Faith Journey through Jesus' Parables.* Faith's Horizons. Grand Rapids: Eerdmans, 1994.

Wheeler, Sondra Ely. *Wealth as Peril and Obligation: The New Testament on Possessions.* Grand Rapids: Eerdmans, 1995.

Wimberly, Norma. *Putting God First: The Tithe.* Camp Hill, Pa.: Christian Publications, 1997.

Wuthnow, Robert. *God and Mammon in America.* New York: The Free Press, 1994.

———. *Poor Richard's Principle: Recovering the American Dream Through the Moral Dimension of Work, Business, and Money.* Princeton: Princeton University Press, 1998.

Also of interest:

Affluenza is a one-hour PBS special that explores the high social and environmental costs of materialism and overconsumption. *Affluenza* profiles people and organizations that are reducing consumption and waste, choosing work that reflects their values, and working to live in better balance with the environment. To order a VHS copy of *Affluenza,* contact Bullfrog Films at 1-800-543-FROG, by e-mail at bullfrog@igc.org, or on the Web at www.bullfrogfilms.com. A teacher's guide and list of resources are available on the Web site.

Stewards of the Good News of Political Communities I

10 Session

Barbara Green
Alan Geyer

Many people think that religion and politics don't mix, but the Bible is filled with passages about the ways that faithful people are stewards of their political communities. The neighborhoods, the towns and cities, and the nations in which we live are communities whose common life is entrusted to our care. As stewards of all God's gifts, we will think together this week and next about the ways that we can care for the life and vitality of those communities.

● ● ●

Is government an expression of human sinfulness or of God's good creation? Or can it have elements of both? Politician jokes are rife in our culture at the beginning of the new century, expressing contempt for political institutions and vocations of public service along the lines of, "Nothing good can come out of Washington." In the context of that prevailing attitude, how are we to understand political community as an expression of the good news of Jesus Christ? Why should the care of God's stewards be "wasted" on down-and-dirty politics?

Read Isaiah 1:12-17
Luke 1:46-55

Politics can, indeed, be down-and-dirty, with money and raw power winning almost every time. But politics as the ordering of human community is the arena in which God calls us to bring justice to all people. The Scripture passages for this session offer God's vision for just community. And so public service can be a high calling. The messy process of coming together is how God intends for us to live. Participating in it is what the stewardship of political community is all about. The Christian ethicist Reinhold Niebuhr used to say that human injustice makes democracy necessary and human goodness makes democracy possible. In that pithy remark he captured both the sinful nature and the potential good of political community.

Stewards in Biblical Times

The Bible offers a host of perspectives on how human communities should be ordered and what their responsibilities and limitations should be. Particularly strong, dramatic expectations of what human community should be come from these texts from Isaiah 1 and Luke 1.

Isaiah 1:12-17 describes God's anger at the Hebrew people who are conducting acts of worship while ignoring the sufferings of others around them. Bringing offerings and conducting solemn assemblies is simply not enough. Appointed festivals are loathsome to God while the people are behaving in evil ways. God will not listen to the people's prayers, no matter how hard they pray. "Your hands are full of blood," God says, "Wash yourselves; make yourselves clean; remove the evil of your doings from before my eyes; cease to do evil, learn to do good" (Isaiah 1:15b-17a). Doing good is made quite explicit: seeking justice, rescuing the oppressed, defending the orphan and widow.

Where in your community do you see God's people paying more attention to "solemn assemblies" than to justice?

God's rejection of these acts of worship should be understood in the context of a broader indictment of Judah's wickedness, which fills the whole first chapter of Isaiah. The whole nation has gone bad. The environment has been destroyed, not tended. The cities are full of corruption and criminals. The leadership is corrupt. Jerusalem, the most beloved and holy city, has degenerated to the point that it is like Sodom and Gomorrah, the most contemptible symbols of evil, and deserves to share their fate. God is furious. Ezekiel 16:49 describes Sodom's decadence thus: "This was the guilt of your sister Sodom: she and her daughters had pride, excess of food, and prosperous ease, but did not aid the poor and needy." For Judah, as for Sodom (as for us?), in God's eyes, all the variety of worship the people come up with will not make up for this fundamental disgrace.

What are some things you see in your community that you think would make God furious?

There are other passages in the Old Testament that are parallel to this clarion call. The most famous is the one from Amos 5:21-24 so often cited by Martin Luther King, Jr.: "I hate, I despise your festivals, and I take no delight in your solemn assemblies ... But let justice roll down like waters, and righteousness like an everflowing stream." An equally important proclamation of a similar theme is the text from Isaiah 61 that Jesus reads when he goes to the temple to preach:

> "The Spirit of the Lord is upon me,
> because he has anointed me
> to bring good news to the poor.

He has sent me to proclaim
release to the captives
and recovery of sight to the blind,
to let the oppressed go free,
to proclaim the year of the Lord's favor."

(Luke 4:18-19)

A fundamental theme of the Old Testament is that the poor may have hope, because God created them for a better life and intends for them to have it.

That hope is strengthened in our New Testament passage. Luke 1:46-55 is commonly called the Magnificat, after its Latin opening line, *Magnificat anima mea Domino.* It is one of the great biblical hymns outside the psalter. In the church traditions that conduct daily vespers, it is sung every day at the evening service. In Luke's Gospel, it is sung by Mary in response to learning that she is to give birth to the Son of God: "My soul magnifies the Lord." Mary trusts the words of this hymn, that what they promise will really come to be. She is speaking directly out of her own experience. She is young, unmarried, female, the lowest of the low in her society, and is about to experience greatness beyond her imagining. The child she will bear will be greater than all others and will transform the whole world.

Mary's song goes on to tell what those transformations will be. God's mercy will be extended to those who fear God. But two pillars of political order will be turned upside down: power and property. The powerful will be deposed, and the lowly will be lifted up. The hungry will be filled with good food, and the rich will learn what it is like to be hungry. In New Testament times, the greatest political power was that of the Roman Empire, whose reach had extended into Palestine. Rome's hierarchy of authorities, the poverty imposed by its taxation system, its bloody repression of any opposition brought a new level of powerlessness to ordinary people in outlying provinces like Palestine. In Jesus' day, hope that the lowly would be lifted up and the hungry filled became very specifically directed toward that oppressive regime.

The bottom line from both these texts? Unjust, inequitable social orders will not stand before God. Period. They will be judged, and they will fall. The poor, the marginalized, the sick, and the oppressed may have real hope because God's anger is directed straight to the forces that do them harm and God's love has a special place for them.

What are some things you see in your community that you think would make God rejoice?

Stewards in History

What do you think Luther would say about our present government?

During the time of the Protestant Reformation both the understanding and practice of civil government took on new dimensions and importance. Until then the papacy claimed divine authority for wielding an enormous amount of wealth and political power. That power was extended over princes and secular rulers and was ferociously competitive with them. The Reformers challenged the Pope's power, and then when papal authority was forced out of a region they had to deal with the power vacuum that remained. In fact, the Reformation often presupposed that only civil governments could reform the Christian church!

Two principal reformers, Martin Luther and John Calvin, both developed extensive theories on civil government, grounded in their concerns for the reform of the church in their regions. Luther developed the idea that there should be two separate "regiments" (he used the word to mean "governments"), one for the secular sphere (the princes) and one for the sacred sphere (the church). The church had no business intervening in matters of the state, and the princes had no business interfering with the structures and governance of the church. Of course, the church that Luther knew was the grasping and corrupted papacy of the late Middle Ages. It made him absolutely furious that Rome claimed all sorts of tithes and taxes from the churches in Germany. When he drew such an impenetrable wall between the secular and sacred, he intended to stop those corrupt practices. He wrote, "The secular authority has the sword and the rod in its hand to punish the evil and protect the righteous."

But Luther also understood that the attributes important in Christianity—humility, forgiveness, charity, pureness of heart, and the like—are not sufficient to organize the authority of a state. He believed that nature and reason, which he called the lower human capacities, were the guiding principles for the state, while the higher human capacities, grace and revelation, were germane to the church. In a sermon on Matthew 12:10, he preached, "Thus in today's gospel passage, we have two worthy, high teachings. First, that Christ is a king of grace and of all consolation, who speaks gently to poor burdened consciences in his gospel, consoles them against sin, and desires to help them to eternal life. For even though strict secular government is also God's reign, it is God's rule only

on the left hand, which will come to an end. God's eternal reign is God's true reign, which comes to us through the Word and draws us into the Word."[1]

A generation after Luther, Calvin emphasized the sovereignty of God over all spheres of life. Thus, for Calvin government had its authority given by God, and the church had a responsibility to see that it functioned in accordance with God's will. In Calvin's Geneva the church was obligated to "meddle in politics!" Calvin developed a more constructive model for government than Luther's: "Civil government has as its appointed end, as long as we live among people, to cherish and protect the outward worship of God, to defend sound doctrine of piety and the position of the church, to adjust our life to the human society, to form our social behavior to civil righteousness, to reconcile us with one another, and to promote general peace and tranquillity."[2] He expected government to protect the special position of the church.

John Wesley was deeply committed to bringing the gospel message to the working classes of eighteenth-century Britain. Although his movement was primarily concerned with spiritual renewal, his moral concerns sometimes led to more systematic attempts to understand poverty and to address its causes. He often expressed outrage over the extreme discrepancies between wealth and poverty around him. He advocated passionately on behalf of relief for the poor, including publicly sponsored relief according to the English "Poor Law" as well as private benevolences.

Wesley showed his ability to analyze the social or systematic causes of poverty in his "Thoughts on the Present Scarcity of Provisions" (1773). Although we would not agree with his view of the American Revolution (he opposed it!), his writings show his concern for citizens' responsibility to their governments. In a very different manner, however, he wrote passionately against slavery, and his last letter was written to William Wilberforce, encouraging Wilberforce's political efforts to secure the abolition of slavery in the British Empire. In this way his moral views extended to influence over political actions.[3]

Stewards in Our Time

As radical as these changes were during the time of the Reformation, they do not reflect the revolutionary upheaval

What do you think Calvin would say about our present government?

If John Wesley were alive today, what might he say and do in your community?

Where do you see the transforming power of Jesus Christ at work in the world?

What are some ways we can work for justice in our communities?

implied in our texts. Liberation theologians in our time have come closer to understanding and applying that radical proclamation turning power structures on their heads. One of the fathers of liberation theology, Gustavo Gutierrez, drew his ideas about liberation from the doctrine of salvation, which is central to the good news of Jesus Christ. For Gutierrez, salvation is not an individualistic, otherworldly agenda to be imposed upon pagan peoples. Instead, it is God's redemptive work both within and beyond human history and takes place for communities as well as individuals. Political liberation is part of God's redemptive work of salvation. At their 1968 Medellín conference, the Latin American Catholic bishops extensively explored similar ideas. They proclaimed that Jesus Christ, by his death and resurrection, transformed human reality and made it possible for us to reach fulfillment as human beings. Such fulfillment included society as well as the individual and called for political transformation of repressive systems.

Significant political changes have occurred in the 1990s in many countries. Eastern European countries have rid themselves of Soviet dominance and gained independence. South Africa has been transformed from the system of apartheid. Some African despots have been deposed. Real liberation and real change has happened in the world. In fear and trembling, we may be bold to say that God's hand has been at work in human history in these changes.

Yet this last decade has seen more than its share of bitter bloodshed in the Persian Gulf War, the terrible civil wars in Sudan, Liberia, Sierra Leone, Rwanda, the Congo, and the Balkans. At home we are plagued with continuing discrimination by the majority population toward minorities: Native Americans, Latino immigrants, African Americans, and too many others to list here. There is a widening gap between the rich and poor in almost all communities. The majority of the world's population continues to live under the most minimal subsistence standards. The vision of Mary's song is a long way from fulfillment.

What do these biblical witnesses have to say to us today? That God is not content with the way the world works. That violence harms God's intent for human community. That the increasingly sharp economic divisions are contrary to God's purposes for the whole human community. That the good news of Jesus Christ is as urgent for us today as it has ever been throughout history.

Becoming Stewards: Understanding the World

Certainly one of the functions of government is to restrain human sinfulness and misdeeds. Criminal laws, police forces, prisons, the military, and much of the judicial system are expressions of the restraining and punitive function of government. Political communities invest that restraining authority in their governments. Unless that restraining authority also includes respect for human rights and law, it will degenerate into totalitarianism, terror, or dictatorships. In our country, we have seen an increasing amount of spending on these restraining functions: police, prisons, and criminal justice.

But a second function of government is a constructive one. Government is not doing its job unless it is building and supporting institutions that enable human community to thrive. Public health systems, medical research, public education, transportation systems, and social service programs all are parts of this constructive function of government. This responsibility of government is a strong element in the biblical perspectives on political community.

If you were mayor of your city, what would you change?

Living in the World

At a recent congregational supper, a woman active in both church and community stood up and cried out: "Why is it that it is harder for me to be honest here in my own church than in any other organization I belong to?" She went on to say that the things she cared about most deeply as a Christian could be discussed more candidly in groups outside the church—issues like poverty and foreign policy. Yes, *political issues.*

For us as Christians, the stewardship of political community rightly begins with forming congregations themselves into peaceable communities in which members are genuinely free to share their deepest concerns and convictions about political issues—prayerfully, thoughtfully, and in the light of biblical faith. Are there arenas for such sharing in your church? Congregations can offer forums for dialogue on the most fateful, troublesome, controversial questions their members must vote and act upon in the political arenas outside the church. Such forums call for a lively program of adult education, the church's own resources of information and intelligence, and an awareness of the

What could you do in your congregation to help make it a place where people are free to share their deepest concerns and convictions about political issues?

public policy positions of the denomination and other Christian groups. Church libraries can serve as active resource and information centers. Find out what resources are available in your library and how you might suggest additional resources. Here are some suggested practices you might engage in as a steward of your political communities:

● **Take time to reflect.** It is important to slow down our lives enough to decide which issues are most important to us. This means taking time to reflect and listen closely. Set aside time to read and think about local political issues.

● **Choose one of your talents to use for God's purposes.** Identify an issue that concerns you, and find out how you might give time and resources in your local community to support it. We all have our own distinct gifts, strengths, and opportunities to make our lives count.

● **Organize an educational event.** Bring a speaker from the community to talk about an important issue. You might do this for an already established group such as your Sunday school class or your women's or men's group. Teaching is a major tool of Christianity.

● **Share stories.** Powerful stories are able to create community. Stories give us images of what is truly worth seeking and worth doing. Encourage people to talk about their political experience.

To live as faithful disciples of Jesus Christ calls for disciplined practices of action outside the walls of the church. There is a world of difference between a congregation of uninvolved, casual spectators and a congregation of active apostles who come together to pray and talk about what it means to be God's stewards when our political involvement can be demanding or discouraging. We will be sustained by worshiping congregations committed to living out God's vision in Mary's song.

1. Martin Luther, Letter to the Christian Nobility of the German Nation, 1520, and Collected Sermons, author's translation.

2. John Calvin, *Calvin: Institutes of the Christian Religion*, ed. John T. McNeill, 2 vols. (Philadelphia: Westminster Press, 1960), II, book 4, chap. 20.

3. Francis John McConnell, *John Wesley* (Nashville: Abingdon Press, 1939), p. 233.

Stewards of the Good News of Political Communities II

Barbara Green
Alan Geyer

Read   Exodus 23:1-12
Matthew 20:
20-28

Many of us have contradictory attitudes and feelings about government and politics. One moment we claim God's providence in the establishment of our nation and divine guidance in the shaping of our unique system of government. But the next moment we may be persuaded that our government is our enemy, that we must get it "off our backs," and that the way to prove our patriotism is to condemn government and all its works. In this latter mood, it isn't easy to think of politics as "good news."

Many of us have strong convictions about the separation of church and state, but we don't agree about what that principle actually means in practice. Does it mean that Christians—or churches—should keep their faith and their politics separate? That religion should "stay out of politics"? Or does it guarantee Christians and their churches the freedom to turn to government to legislate on moral issues, such as civil rights, poverty, pornography, or abortion? Is Christian faith essentially a private matter that should not intrude upon political controversies?

The overwhelming testimony of Scripture, especially in the Old Testament prophets and the teaching of Jesus, is that religion cannot be faithfully divorced from politics. At the core of our biblical faith is the affirmation that power must be exercised on behalf of justice. Whatever else justice means, it is the foundation of political community.

Stewards in Biblical Times

A main theme in the Old Testament is the increasing sensitivity on the part of the Hebrew community to God's desire for justice, or *mishpat* in Hebrew. The awareness of the people moves from a very primitive level to a very lofty one.

We can see how the understanding of justice changes through the Scriptures, as the people become more aware of God's vision for human community. One early image is *unlimited revenge* in response to injury or injustice. In Genesis

How do you define justice?

4:23-24, Lamech talks tough to his wives: "Listen to what I say: I have killed a man for wounding me, a young man for striking me. If Cain is avenged sevenfold, truly Lamech seventy-sevenfold."

Then comes a more carefully calculated sense of justice as *limited and proportional retaliation,* as in Exodus 21:23-25. If someone is harmed, "then you shall give life for life, eye for eye, tooth for tooth, hand for hand, foot for foot, burn for burn, wound for wound, stripe for stripe."

But then in Deuteronomy 32:35, revenge and even limited retaliation seem to be prohibited because God has exclusive jurisdiction in such matters: "Vengeance is mine," says the Lord.

These texts focus on personal conduct and negative notions of justice. The more positive imperatives of justice that are found in many other biblical passages tell us of God's desire for human community.

The first dozen verses of Exodus 23 clearly presuppose the political institutions required to make justice a reality: (1) an ordered community, (2) an equitable rule of law for both citizens and aliens, and (3) a system of government with executive, legislative, and judicial functions. This passage suggests that political communities and their governing institutions are part of God's intentions for our common life with and for one another.

If that is true—if indeed government is grounded in God's good creation—then the stewardship of political community requires respecting and supporting the legitimate functions of government, honoring the vocations of legislators and bureaucrats and police and judges and diplomats, and resisting those forces that tend to weaken the capacity of government to do justice and serve the common good.

What is especially remarkable about Exodus 23 is that it shows us a highly complex society, with elaborate governing and legal institutions, perhaps by the thirteenth century before the birth of Jesus, well over three thousand years ago. All the human relationships of the political community are to be shaped by the positive obligations of justice.

These verses call for the moral integrity of both government and citizens. Civic life must not be corrupted by "false reports" or by an evil conspiracy making a "malicious witness" (no mud slinging!). The passage reflects obvious

In what ways do our political systems measure up to God's commandments in this passage from Exodus?

experience of the ways in which bribery can corrupt the administration of government and "subverts the cause of those who are in the right." There is awareness of the ways in which a political majority may tyrannously override the rights of minorities. Not only is there respect for property rights, there is an imperative to return missing property (like a stray ox or donkey), even to one's personal enemy. Courts must function with absolute impartiality. Aliens are to be treated with respect because the people of Israel "know the heart of an alien, for you were aliens in the land of Egypt" (Exodus 23:9).

God's justice is thus concerned with the well-being of the whole community and all its creatures. It is an expression of the love of God in covenant relationship with the human community. At the highest levels of Old Testament law and prophecy, *mishpat* becomes *shalom:* wholeness, health, and harmony in all human relationships. Justice is the structure of human rights and responsibilities that best expresses God's covenant-love.

In Matthew 20:20-28, Jesus takes our understanding of God's vision for human community even further. Jesus is confronted by the mother of James and John, two of his disciples, seeking special status and privileges for her two sons in the coming kingdom. Jesus could not and would not grant such favors. He then explains to the other ten disciples (who had heard this special pleading and became angry) that the seeking of exalted status and power is not only contrary to the ways of his kingdom: the kingdom's style of leadership is to be the servant of the people, not their master—much less their tyrant.

Taken together, Exodus 23 and Matthew 20 affirm the necessity of government, to assure equity, as well as the mission of government, to bring wholeness, health, and harmony to human relationships and to serve the ends of equity and community well-being. Such a perspective rejects both anarchy (no government at all) and tyranny (oppressive government).

Stewards in History

The biblical understanding of community life calls for high standards for the ways the churches should engage political institutions. The historic record of the churches at best is mixed. Prior to the eighteenth century neither church

Where are some places you see political systems working for the well-being of the whole community?

In what ways do you think our government undercuts the church, and in what ways do you think it supports the church?

hierarchies nor theologians advocated a fully democratic viewpoint in which human rights are the foundation of political authority. Moreover, virtually every form of Christianity has been both the victim and the perpetrator of discrimination, persecution, and violence against other Christians and non-Christians.

The earliest Christian generations were persecuted by a Roman Empire that practiced emperor-worship. A great turnabout occurred in the fourth century when Emperor Constantine decreed that Christianity should be tolerated within the Empire. (Constantine himself supported Christian churches and was baptized shortly before he died.) Three centuries later, Pope Gregory the Great had acquired such power that he proclaimed the church's supreme authority over the governments within its reach and even acted in civil defense of the city of Rome. It might be important to remember, however, that precisely from the time of Constantine, some Christians rejected the accumulation of possessions and of secular power and began to form monastic communities. The monks' witness was very powerful in the Middle Ages, although monastic movements themselves typically went through phases of accumulation followed by attempts to restore the primitive simplicity and austerity of Christian monasticism.

Despite the witness of the monks, however, the great Catholic medieval vision of universal authority and social harmony often served in practice to rationalize serfdom, severe inequalities, and both religious and political repression. The church itself and many monastic communities came to possess vast lands and great wealth.

In the sixteenth century, the Protestant Reformation arose in protest against the autocratic power and corruption of the church. Martin Luther gave great impetus to the struggle for religious freedom (especially the inner freedom of faith and conscience), but he maintained a repressive attitude toward social change and expressed anti-Semitic sentiments that would echo tragically four centuries later in Nazi Germany.

John Calvin's Geneva offered a somewhat different religio-political model that, in practice, was also repressive: a *theocracy* in which an established church dominated the government, compelled obedience to one creed, and resorted to burning heretics at the stake. Later generations

of Calvinists, however, would bring their reforming zeal to the protection of civil liberties, including religious freedom.

The Reformation also gave rise to more radical sects— Anabaptists and Quakers—that rejected all religious establishments and sought to withdraw from all political and military establishments. Lutheran and Calvinist authorities, however, persecuted the leaders of these sects. When Massachusetts Puritan governors banished Roger Williams in 1635 for his Anabaptist convictions, they unwittingly set the stage for the founding of Baptist churches on the American continent, and Baptists would become the most persistent advocates of religious freedom and the separation of church and state.

In the politics of the eighteenth century, the unfolding American experiment of separation of church and state must be understood largely as a reaction against the various church establishments, whether Roman Catholic, Anglican, Lutheran, or Calvinist. Thomas Jefferson regarded his authorship of the Virginia Statute for Religious Freedom as one of his most important lifetime achievements: a victory over the intolerant and repressive Anglican establishment in the colony of Virginia.

The constitutional disestablishment of religion in America has not prevented some groups in every generation from attempting to claim that this is a "Christian nation" and to legislate special symbols and requirements in schools and other public places—typically challenged by Jewish leaders and civil liberties organizations. In contemporary America, the rapid growth of Muslim, Hindu, Buddhist, and other non-Christian religions has made this country and its government the world's most extraordinary proving ground for peaceful pluralism and the fullness of religious freedom.

We might note on this matter that although U.S. Courts made it clear from the 1960s that religious rituals (or prayers) could not be imposed in public schools or other institutions, they actually suggested that religious traditions *should* be taught publicly. Unfortunately, we have developed very few models for the teaching of religious traditions; indeed, many public schools and their textbooks shy away from even the mention of religious topics. That can lead to some startling anomalies, such as school textbook descriptions of the work of the Reverend Martin Luther King, Jr. that never mention his religious commitments or his role as a Baptist pastor.

What are some new issues we face because of our growing religious diversity?

Stewards in Our Time

In what ways do you think churches should be involved in political issues?

Because many of them had experienced religious persecution in the countries they came from, the founders of the United States were determined to protect the freedom of religion. Sometimes we have misunderstood that protection to be the freedom "from" religion but that was never their intent. They saw religious faith of many varieties as being an important part of community life. American political culture has been partly shaped by the commitment to that experiment begun at a time when national religions were the norm.

In our time we have significant differences of opinion about the role of the church in politics. Churches are not permitted to endorse particular parties or candidates for office, but they are free to discuss and take positions on issues facing the community and the nation. Some Christians believe that political issues should never be discussed at church, while others see their faith and their political activity as very closely related. This can be a source of tension in our congregations. In addition, tension sometimes arises in our communities over differing religious beliefs and practices. A hundred or even fifty years ago the communities in which we lived were much more homogeneous. But our culture has become increasingly pluralistic, and we find our neighborhoods are becoming more and more diverse. Our children are going to school with Muslim and Hindu children as well as Christian and Jewish children.

Even if we believe that our faith is related to our politics, sometimes we are tempted to retreat from political conversation and action when we see abuses of power and promotion of self-interest all around us. But the Scripture texts for this session indicate that God is indeed interested in the way we live together—the way we organize our government and our political life and the way we handle power. As Christians we are called to be stewards of our political life. If we believe that the government should be working for the common good that will lead us to a positive understanding of the potential role of politics.

In the Gospels Jesus has given us a vision of what the reign of God will be like. It is the common ground for Christians who are called to make possible tomorrow what seems impossible today. Implicit in the commandments that

we love both God and neighbor is a call for us to live in community with one another, a community that reflects the love that God has shown for us. The means by which such communities are developed and shaped is through politics—the development of governments that seek to bring the community closer to our vision of it as healthy and whole. As people and their governments become increasingly connected across the globe, we can claim what we discover in the Scriptures: that God is Creator of all people and all nations and sometimes even works through our enemies, whom we are called to love and forgive. Jesus Christ is the Prince of Peace who breaks down the dividing walls of hostility. The biblical vision of a New Earth in which all people come together peaceably before God and in which there is no more hunger or hurt or sorrow is the vision toward which we are called to work.

What do you think will be the characteristics of God's reign? List them.

Becoming Stewards: Understanding the World

If we are to be stewards of the political communities of which we are a part, we cannot sit back and let others take responsibility for our common life. Fewer and fewer people even bother to vote, much less participate in political activity in their communities. And yet we all long for political leaders who will help build community and will bring people together for projects that promote the common good. We know that finding workable solutions to the problems we face is a difficult task but we also know that there are others like us who want to respond to a larger vision that gives us a sense of purpose and meaning.

What are some characteristics of good stewards of political life?

The good news of the gospel was not offered only to a deserving few, but to all people. As Christians we believe that we have been made in the image of God and that God intends for us wholeness and well-being. And so our concern must always be for the needs of the stranger, the one who is different from us. We see the needs in many places—homeless people, millions without health care, violence on our streets and in our schools, domestic abuse, the breakdown of the family, youth at risk, hungry children, victims of hate crimes. For all of these we need a new vision for our communities that will transcend both liberal and conservative categories and bring us together to work for justice and peace for everyone in the community.

When we remember God's great love for us and the

claims that the gospel makes on us, we begin asking questions about what we might do to live more faithfully as God's stewards in the political arena. We won't all agree. The causes that matter most to us will differ and so will our decisions about how to engage those causes. But if we struggle together we will find a common sense of purpose and hope, and our voices can be powerful.

Living in the World

List the issues in your community that concern you the most.

As we begin to think of specific ways that we can be stewards of our political communities, it is important to remember that, while no one of us can respond alone, each of us has some power to act, and history shows us over and over that together we can make a difference. The first step is becoming aware of the injustices that are within our reach. What can you do to become more aware of these issues in your community? As citizens in a free society, we have genuine power in local, state, and national political organizations and through them in the international arena.

Local organizations, town councils, zoning boards, and the like, make significant decisions every day. They affect the location and availability of housing for the working poor, and so indirectly also the quality of schooling available to their children. They determine where public and commercial facilities will be placed and who will bear the burdens of air, water, and soil pollution. They often decide whether facilities will be built to help the most vulnerable, the homeless, and the mentally ill. Public opinion is very important to organizations, and they will respond when we express ourselves. By attending meetings and learning about the issues, you can have an effect on decisions in your community. Choose one area as a beginning place and participate in public events.

State representatives depend upon the support of voters, and they will listen as they create economic policies that determine who gets help and how. This includes access to education, health care, child care, employment assistance, and protection against violence and unjust discrimination. Even at the national level, congressional representatives cannot afford to ignore the expressed opinion of their constituents. Legislative aides report that they routinely assume that fifty more constituents share the view of every private opinion letter they receive, since most people will not bother to write.

Too often we find it easy to express public disdain for politicians and complain the government is unresponsive, but at the same time we remain disengaged from the political process and often let our power go unused. This, too, is a failure in stewardship. As God's steward you can talk to others about issues and encourage them to get involved.

Alongside our effective participation in government, another way we can act as stewards is to create and support institutions that protect and empower those who are victims of injustice. Advocacy and support groups meet a wide range of needs, from housing and health care to protection from abuse and exploitation. Most of these organizations depend on the labor and dedication of people like you and me. Choose an organization that is working in an area important to you. Find out how you can volunteer to help support their work. Here we can find rich opportunities to make the gospel of Jesus Christ real in the lives of the neediest, and we can experience enormous joy and spiritual growth as a result.

If we are to be personally engaged in our political communities, we must become educated about political issues. Fortunately, we are not left to analyze these complex problems on our own. A number of Christian, interfaith, and secular organizations exist to help us understand the problems and needs that must be addressed in our communities. Most of these focus on some particular area of concern, for example, the well-being of children, the problem of hunger, or the plight of refugees. In this age of information, a simple search of your local library or the Internet can put you in touch with information and expert help so that your engagement can be well informed and effective. Locate some of these resources and share them with your group.

It is important to know the particular perspective of these groups so that you will have confidence in the information they provide. Followers of Jesus Christ will sometimes disagree about what political engagement is faithful to the Gospel. Congregations are the natural place to begin our self-education as responsible participants in our wider society. Many organizations have materials prepared specifically for use in worship and Christian education settings. Identify a time when your congregation might focus on a particular issue in worship or an educational setting and make plans to carry this out. We all may find it difficult at

What are the ways that you intend to get involved in the coming weeks?

times to decide what action God's faithful stewards would take, but as Christians in a democratic society we must remember that when we are faced with injustice, silence is also a political activity.

Working together on these issues in congregations where people differ in their political perspectives is not easy. But churches need to support the involvement of their members in ways that transcend political partisanship. Our churches are also called to nurture some of our members for vocations of public service—educators, bureaucrats, judges, prosecutors, police, public defenders, social workers, military, media—and then celebrate such vocations in our sanctuaries. The stewardship of political communities ultimately requires a faith perspective that views politics as holy ground.

Suggestions for Further Reading

Barndt, Joseph. *Dismantling Racism: The Continuing Challenge to White America.* Minneapolis: Augsburg Fortress Press, 1991.

Dunning, H. Ray. *Reflecting the Divine Image: Christian Ethics in Wesleyan Perspective.* Westmont, Ill.: InterVarsity Press, 1998.

Geyer, Alan. *Ideology in America: Challenges to Faith.* Louisville: Westminster John Knox Press, 1997.

Grenz, Stanley. *The Moral Quest: Foundations of Christian Ethics.* Westmont, Ill.: InterVarsity Press, 1997.

Kosmin, Barry A., and Seymour P. Lachman. *One Nation Under God: Religion in Contemporary American Society.* New York: Crown, 1993.

Loeb, Paul Rogat. *Soul of a Citizen: Living with Conviction in a Cynical Time.* New York: St. Martins Press, 1999.

Marty, Martin E. *Politics, Religion, and the Common Good.* San Francisco: Jossey-Bass, 2000.

McClain, George D., and Walter Wink. *Claiming All Things for God: Prayer, Discernment, and Ritual for Social Change.* Nashville: Abingdon Press, 1998.

Messer, Donald E. *Christian Ethics and Political Action.* Valley Forge, Pa.: Judson Press, 1984.

Mott, Stephen Charles. *A Christian Perspective on Political Thought.* London: Oxford University Press, 1993.

Palmer, Parker J. *The Company of Strangers: Christians and the Renewal of America's Public Life.* New York: Crossroads Press, 1993.

Recinos, Harold J. *Jesus Weeps: Global Encounters on Our Doorstep.* Nashville: Abingdon Press, 1992.

Stackhouse, Max L.; Peter L. Berger; and Dennis P. McCann. *Christian Social Ethics in a Global Era.* Abingdon Press Studies in Christian Ethics and Economic Life, vol. 1. Nashville: Abingdon Press, 1995.

Wallis, Jim. *The Soul of Politics: Discovering a Practical and Prophetic Vision for Change.* Eugene, Ore.: Harvest House, 1995.

Wogoman, J. Philip. *Christian Perspectives on Politics.* Louisville: Westminster John Knox Press, 2000.

Wuthnow, Robert. *Acts of Compassion: Caring for Others and Helping Ourselves.* Princeton: Princeton University Press, 1991.

Yoder, John Howard. *The Politics of Jesus: Vicit Agnus Noster.* Grand Rapids: Eerdmans, 1972.

Also of interest:

The ecumenical Churches' Center for Theology and Public Policy, based at Wesley Theological Seminary in Washington, D.C., exists to help churches with resources that connect faith and politics. *Shalom Papers* is a quarterly journal published by the Center at 4500 Massachusetts Avenue, Washington, D.C., 20016. For more information, visit their Web site at www.wesleysem.edu/Programs/cctpp.asp.

Stewards of Hope: Remembering and Visioning

Bruce C. Birch

This week concludes our study about how we can live as faithful disciples of Jesus Christ and stewards of all God's gifts. In this final week we will think together about what it means to be stewards of the hope we have in God. All of the things that we have discussed during the past weeks come together in this session. We will share with one another the ways we intend to live as God's stewards into the future that God has promised.

Read   *Isaiah 51:1-2*
Psalm 136
Jeremiah 29:4-7, 11-14
Revelation 21:1-7

• • •

Encompassing all of the gifts God has given into our care as stewards is the gift of time—the framework of our days. All of the aspects of our life as God's stewards require the stewardship of our time. Yet, in our modern world, time is often what is least available and often the first thing we squander. The psalmist prays, "So teach us to count our days that we may gain a wise heart" (Psalm 90:12). Faithful caring for the time God has given us is the focus of the last session of our study on the role of the God's steward.

For God's people, time is not an abstract, neutral concept. As God's gift, time has a moral quality. In Genesis 1, every day of creation and what is encompassed by it is declared *good*. At the end of God's creative work, the whole of those days is pronounced *very good* (Genesis 1:31), and a sabbath day is set aside to remember and commemorate the goodness of God's creation. The structure of our week reminds us of the goodness God intends for our days in the midst of creation.

Thus, time for the community of God's stewards is not merely the quantity of our days. Time for the community of God's stewards has a quality—it is the quality of hope. Our knowledge that time is God's gift intended for our good makes us hopeful even in the midst of days of crisis. Hope is the confidence that time is in God's hands and that our past, present, and future are filled with God's possibilities for wholeness even in the midst of brokenness. As stewards of time we are also stewards of hope. To lose sight of this in moments of despair is to lose touch with the very gift of our life.

Name some times when it has been difficult for you to be hopeful.

Stewards in Biblical Times

What enables hope? In the biblical story we often learn of hope from the ancient community's own struggle with hopelessness. One of those particular times was the experience of Israel in Babylonian exile. In 587 B.C., a Babylonian army broke through the walls of Jerusalem, destroyed the Temple, ended the Davidic kingship, and carried most of the citizens away into exile in Babylon. The prophets had warned Israel that arrogant and self-centered leadership, national pride, social injustice, and idolatrous loyalties were leading the nation toward disaster. Now, all that gave life meaning and value lay in shambles, and the people feared that even God had been defeated or had abandoned them. The despairing voice of Psalm 137 cries out: "How shall we sing the Lord's song in a strange land?" The implied answer is that there is no singing of the Lord's song in the midst of hopelessness.

Remarkably, three great voices rise in songs of hope during this very time of exile despair: the prophets Jeremiah, Ezekiel, and the prophet of Isaiah 40–55 that we call Deutero-Isaiah. They were singers in the midst of the nonsingers. They spoke of hope to those who had given up hope. What enabled them to be hopeful when others despaired, and how can we live all of our days as stewards of hope?

1. Hope is grounded first of all in **memory**. Those who would be stewards of hope must remember what God has done and how faithful people have responded to God's action. In Isaiah 51:1b-2a the prophet declares to the exiles in Babylon, "Look to the rock from which you were hewn, and to the quarry from which you were dug. Look to Abraham your father and to Sarah who bore you." He calls the nonsingers in Babylon to remember their own story beginning with Abraham and Sarah. Psalm 136 is a responsive hymn that tells the story of God's creation and salvation, proclaiming that God's "steadfast love endures forever."

It is memory that gives the community of faith its identity. Without memory, the community is rootless and afraid that God is absent or uncaring in their time of need. Hope cannot flourish where memory is not renewed and claimed. In both the Old and New Testament, memory focuses

What are some memories you have of God's steadfast love and action in your life?

around God's salvation. Israel is asked to "remember that you were a slave in the land of Egypt, and the LORD your God redeemed you" (Deuteronomy 15:15). In his Pentecost sermon, Peter proclaims, "Jesus of Nazareth, a man attested to you by God with deeds of power, wonders, and signs that God did through him among you, . . . God raised him up, having freed him from death, because it was impossible for him to be held in its power" (Acts 2:22, 24). Hope is grounded in knowing that God has already redeemed us.

2. Memory alone is not enough. Hope is also grounded in **vision**, the confidence that our future is in God's hands. Knowing what God has done allows us to anticipate with hope what God yet can do. In Isaiah 43:19, the prophet who called exiles to remember also says to them, "I [God] am about to do a new thing; now it springs forth, do you not perceive it?" The prophet Jeremiah writes a letter to the exiles in Babylon and encourages them to look ahead in hope rather than despair, "For surely I know the plans I have for you, says the LORD, plans for your welfare and not for harm, to give you a future with hope" (Jeremiah 29:11). Hopeful vision orients the community of faith to mission. God calls us from the present with its contentments and crises into new futures for the sake of participating in God's ongoing purposes for our lives and the life of the world. Memory helps us discern the future to which God is calling us.

The biblical story gives us confidence and hope for the immediate future, but it also gives us a long-term vision of God's future. As Christians today we can live hopefully into the immediate future because the Bible gives us a vision that God's kingdom of love, peace, and justice will finally come in its fullness. Our immediate future is one further step toward the fulfillment of God's redeeming purposes for all of history. To know and believe that God is at work to bring the world to the final fullness of salvation gives us hope that God has new things in store for our own futures. In God the future is always filled with hopeful possibilities no matter how difficult the present might be.

3. Identity rooted in memory and mission rooted in vision can free us from the tyranny of the present so that we can live as hopeful people. Hopeful **witness** in the present depends on our freedom from the despair that cannot see

What vision do you have of where God is calling you in the future?

beyond our present crises or the complacency that comes from living in the self-interest of the moment. Memory and vision allow us as God's people to witness to hopeful possibilities in every present circumstance. Jeremiah's letter to the Babylonian exiles calls them to this task by speaking of the possibilities for wholeness we must seek in the times and places given to us. The Hebrew word for wholeness is *shalom,* and it is translated here as "welfare": "Seek the welfare of the city where I have sent you into exile, and pray to the LORD on its behalf, for in its welfare you will find your welfare" (Jeremiah 29:7). Even when we are in crisis, if we refuse to be cut off from hopeful memory or blinded to hopeful vision then we can claim and witness to the hopeful possibilities of the present. Jeremiah's letter urges the exiles to claim the fullness of faithful life even in Babylon (29:4-6).

The God we know in Jesus Christ is the God of past, present, and future. All time is encompassed by God's purpose. That is what empowers God's people to live constantly as hopeful people—even in crises such as exile. If we are to be stewards of time, we must also be stewards of hope. In God's providence all times are hope-filled. The words of the prophet to the exiles in Isaiah 40:28, 31 also address us as exiles in our own time: "Have you not known? Have you not heard? The LORD is the everlasting God, the Creator of the ends of the earth [i.e., the God of all times and places]...those who wait for the LORD shall renew their strength, they shall mount up with wings like eagles, they shall run and not be weary, they shall walk and not faint."

Stewards in History

Hope cannot endure in the abstract. Hope requires hopeful practices and communities that nourish memory and renew vision. We could not hear the hopeful voices from the biblical communities during the Babylonian exile or the struggles of the early church apart from generations who handed on God's hopeful word and lived in ways that made hope visible.

During the Babylonian exile, several practices emerged that demonstrate for us the stewardship of hope. These continued and were expanded or adapted by the early church and have endured through history to the present. These practices can be named as **Scripture, sabbath, and synagogue.**

1. With the destruction of the Temple and the dispersal of Israel's leadership, Babylonian exile threatened the identity and survival of God's people descended from the promise to Abraham. The story of God's people could have been lost. There were some written materials, but most was oral tradition. It was during and after the exile that *written Scripture* began to make its appearance. When Ezra returned to beleaguered Jerusalem from Babylon, he brought with him a law book that he read to the assembled people (Nehemiah 8:1-8). This was probably the first appearance of the Torah, the first five books of our Bible. In the years that followed, additional collections of testimony were written down—first the prophets, then the writings.

In the early church following the life, ministry, death, and resurrection of Jesus, written testimony began to appear. First the letters of Paul and other early church leaders appeared, then gospel accounts of the life and teachings of Jesus, accounts and writings of the early church, and finally the great vision of Revelation. The early church also accepted the earlier Scripture collections of Israel as their Scripture and refused to follow those who would separate them.

Bible reading and Bible study thus became centrally important practices for early Jews and Christians as a way to preserve memory and renew the community's vision. To care for the gift of God's written word became a practice that enabled the stewardship of hope through ongoing generations.

Name some times when the Bible has been a source of hope for you.

2. The *observance of the sabbath* also became a very important practice at the time of the Babylonian exile. Sabbath observance did not begin at this time. It was known and practiced in early periods in Israel's life, but during exile the rhythm of pausing every seventh day to acknowledge God's gifts became especially important to a people who feared that God's gifts had been lost to them.

It is interesting to notice that Israel had two different but complementary reasons for observing sabbath. The Ten Commandments are found both in Exodus 20 and in Deuteronomy 5. In each place the observance of sabbath is one of the foundational commandments for God's covenant people. But in each place a different meaning is attached. In Exodus it is to remind us of the creation when God rested on the seventh day. In Deuteronomy it is a remembrance that we were once slaves in Egypt and the Lord delivered us.

What are some ways that you observe sabbath, and why are they important?

These testimonies remind us of God's gifts in two different dimensions. In creation we are reminded of God's universal gifts to all of creation—gifts of life and potential for wholeness and well-being. In the deliverance from Egypt we are reminded of the gift of God's salvation that called into being the covenant people of which we are still a part—a gift of new life possible out of every brokenness and a gift of ongoing covenant relationship with God. In sabbath we remember both the universal and the particular gifts of God's grace. When we practice sabbath we interrupt the flow of the world's time to acknowledge the overriding importance of God's gifts in the midst of our worldly possessions and loyalties.

What are some ways that worshiping in the community helps sustain you through the week?

3. With the Temple destroyed, the people of Israel in Babylon had no gathering place for their traditions and observances. Although its origins are not entirely known, we do know that it is during this time of exile and its aftermath that the *synagogue* developed as a center of Scripture reading, prayer, praise, and community support among the Jews dispersed throughout the world. Even after the Temple was rebuilt, local synagogues continued as a central element of Jewish life, and early Christian churches were deeply influenced by the practices of the synagogue. In many ways, the synagogue is the ancestor of the local congregation.

The synagogue created a rhythm of gathering and dispersing as the people of God that is at the heart of our faith experience as Christians. It works with sabbath and Scripture since sabbath is the time set aside for gathering and Scripture reading is a primary activity of the gathered community. That rhythm of gathering together and dispersing into the world as the people of God has continued to mark the life of the church throughout its history. It gives all of our days a distinctive quality as God's stewards.

As God's covenant people, a community of stewards and disciples of Jesus Christ, we gather to remember and celebrate the hopeful history of God's salvation. We read and interpret Scripture; we hear the proclamation of God's word for our own time; we offer praise and thanksgiving for all that God has done; we share our burdens with God and with one another. The rhythm of weekly gathering reaffirms

our relationship with God and with one another in God's community.

Yet, the covenant people of God gather for the sake of dispersing into the world. The prayers of the gathered community are not only for personal and community needs but also for the sake of blessing to "all the families of the earth" (Genesis 12:3). Gathering is not an end in itself but enables us to carry the good news of Jesus Christ into the world. Thus, the synagogue and its successor local congregations through the ages become a way of organizing our use of time for the sake of memory and vision—identity and mission.

The exact form of Christian congregations has varied greatly through history, but at their heart all share much in common with the gathering and dispersing rhythms that the synagogue established—gathering for Scripture, prayer, and praise; dispersing to live as God's stewards. Sometimes the gathering was in large communities in great sanctuaries or cathedrals; at other times in house churches or simple chapels. Sometimes the dispersal to mission created great movements, reformations, or revivals; at other times it was the simple witness of faithful disciples.

The early Methodist societies in John Wesley's day organized as class meetings to sustain one another in discipleship. These class meetings were for the purpose of giving account to one another of their Christian discipleship and to sustain one another in their witness. This included an accounting for "works of mercy" through which Christ is served in the world (e.g., feeding the hungry, clothing the naked, visiting the prisons or hospitals, and seeking out those in need). It also included an accounting for "works of piety" such as prayer, searching the Scriptures, the Lord's Supper, fasting, and Christian conference (conversation about the will of God). Other denominational traditions had their own forms of gathering and dispersing that encouraged their members and gave account for the life required of God's covenant people. These are all forms of organizing God's gift of time to enable us to become stewards of all of God's gifts and ultimately stewards of hope.

Stewards in Our Time

Like many generations before us, we know ourselves to be a generation of exiles sharing much in common with our

Name some "works of mercy" that you have done recently.

Name some "works of piety" that you have done recently.

ancestors who thought they could never sing the Lord's song by the rivers in Babylon.

Our sense of dislocation may not be geographic but instead it may be the loss of meaning and hope experienced in countless individual and societal ways. It is the experience of the times when the Lord's song seems impossible or irrelevant. Consider some of the following elements of the mood of exile in our time.

What signs of exile—loss of hope—do you see around you?

- We live in an age often captured and tyrannized by the present. "The future is now!" "Live for the moment!" are popular sentiments. We have been called an age of instant gratification. Consumerism as a way of life is fed by this relentless focus on the now. And when we face a crisis, we have nothing to fall back on.

- Many people in our time have a vision of the future that is primarily one of self-interest. A vision that includes the well-being of others is becoming more difficult to maintain. In the church, individualist forms of piety and religion are extremely popular. Even in congregational life, we sometimes find it difficult to see beyond our local interests. When our dreams narrow to self-interest, we are looking out only for our own survival, an understandable but ultimately defeating strategy against the uncertainties we face.

Where in your life do time pressures make it most difficult for you to remember and pay attention to God?

- There are many signs that we have lost the sense that time is a sacred gift of God. The loss of sabbath observance is more profound than the collapse of blue laws or the intrusion of Little League onto Sunday morning. The loss of sabbath involves our loss of a sense of God's presence in the midst of our time schedules. We give time to God when there is time left over, rather than organizing our lives around a discipline of recognizing God's presence at the center of our lives.

Becoming Stewards of the Gospel: Understanding and Living in the World

The call to be God's stewards encompasses every dimension of our lives as we care for all of God's gifts to us. The role of steward extends from our role as part of God's entire creation, to our part in all the relationships of our lives, to the personal care of our own body, mind, and spirit.

It is appropriate that this final session focus on God's gift of time and its quality of hope because all of the contexts we have been discussing ultimately come down to how we use the time God has given us and whether we will be bringers of hope. Hope is related in our Scripture and tradition to life, salvation, newness, possibility, and wholeness. In every arena considered in this study the steward seeks to enable these qualities. Ultimately all stewardship is the stewardship of hope. All time for God's stewards is less about the duration of our days than about the quality of hope we invest in each moment.

At the conclusion of our journey through these sessions we ask you to reflect on the challenge to be stewards of hope.

- **In our personal lives**—Have we undertaken disciplines and given time to make ourselves hope-filled stewards? Do we adequately care for our bodies, our minds, and our spirits? Many of us simply let time and events flow around or over us, struggling to respond. Such a reactive use of time cannot become hope-filled. In his widely read book *Celebration of Discipline*, Richard Foster suggests a variety of disciplines that can help us become stewards of time and hope rather than simply reacting to the flow of daily events. He discusses inward disciplines (meditation, prayer, fasting, study), outward disciplines (simplicity, solitude, submission, service), and corporate disciplines (confession, worship, guidance, celebration). Choosing a pattern of personal discipline is a first step to new awareness that time is the hope-filled gift of God.

- **In our lives as congregations**—We must ask if our congregational life truly nurtures memory and kindles vision so that we can live as disciples of Jesus Christ. Are we mired in issues of the present or settling for survival? Do we understand ourselves as God's covenant people or simply a part of the local culture? Many churches make the mistake of treating memory and vision as interest areas—Bible study on one side, mission groups on the other. Some treat worship or Bible study as an end in itself, and others are so busy in mission that they have no roots in Scripture and prayer. Memory empowers us for mission, and vision needs roots in the tradition to discern God's future. The rhythms of congregational life should give us opportunities for remembrance, reflection, and celebration

Name some practices you want to try that will support your living as a steward:

. . . in your personal life.

. . . in the life of your congregation.

...in your relationships with others.

and should challenge us to move into the world as witnesses for Jesus Christ, agents for justice, and bringers of life and wholeness. This requires that we share with one another and hold each other accountable for living as God's stewards.

● **In our relationship with others, locally and globally**—Do we use our time in ways that fill our relationships with the hopeful possibilities of God's future? Or do we find ourselves operating primarily out of self-interest? Are we driven by time as the rush of events day after day rather than the gift of God within which relationships are nurtured? Oddly enough, it may be our relationships in the world that would be most affected by reclaiming the sabbath. To set aside some of our time as a reminder of God's time helps us appreciate life as God's gift rather than manipulate life as a product. Relationships are valued for their intrinsic worth rather than their utility. Stewards of hope know that when we give time back to God, we recognize the God-given possibility in every moment and the relationships that fill those moments. Instead of being driven to manage our time, God asks us to trustfully receive all the hopeful possibilities in the gift of our days.

God has given us the gift of all creation, all relationships, and all time. And God has entrusted these gifts into our hands as stewards, representatives of God's own sovereignty over all things. If we were left alone in this task it might indeed overwhelm us. But our faith is that God did not create and withdraw. God has been with us since the beginning of time—giving promises, bringing deliverance, calling us to community, judging and forgiving, renewing and redeeming, and finally, taking flesh in Jesus Christ to overcome death with life. As stewards for such a God, we cannot help but be stewards of hope for all of our days.

Suggestions for Further Reading

Brueggemann, Walter. *Cadences of Home: Preaching Among Exiles.* Louisville: Westminster John Knox Press, 1997.

————. *Interpretation and Obedience: From Faithful Reading to Faithful Living.* Minneapolis: Fortress Press, 1991.

Foster, Richard J. *Celebration of Discipline: The Path to Spiritual Growth.* San Francisco: Harper & Row, 1988.

————. *Freedom of Simplicity.* San Francisco: Harper & Row, 1998.

Job, Rueben, and Norman Shawchuck. *A Guide to Prayer for All God's People.* Nashville: Upper Room Books, 1994.

Jones, Clifford A., ed. *From Proclamation to Practice: A Unique African American Approach to Stewardship.* Valley Forge, Pa.: Judson Press, 1993.

Madigan, Dan. *Many Hands, Many Miracles: Building a Social Service Agency That Works.* Notre Dame, Ind: University of Notre Dame, 1997.

McNamara, Patrick. *More Than Money: Portraits of Transformative Stewardship.* Bethesda, Md.: The Alban Institute, 1999.

Schut, Michael, ed. *Simpler Living, Compassionate Life: A Christian Perspective.* Harrisburg, Pa.: Morehouse Publishing, 1999.

Vallet, Ronald E. *Stepping Stones of the Steward: A Faith Journey Through Jesus' Parables.* Faith's Horizons. Grand Rapids: Eerdmans, 1994.

Willard, Dallas. *The Divine Conspiracy: Rediscovering Our Hidden Life in God.* San Francisco: Harper & Row, 1998.

Also of interest:

Alternatives for Simple Living is a nonprofit organization that equips people of faith to challenge consumerism, live justly, and celebrate responsibly. Started in 1973 as a protest against the commercialization of Christmas, their focus is on encouraging celebrations that reflect conscientious ways of living. They can be reached at 800-821-6153 or through their Web site, www.simpleliving.org.

WRITERS

Bruce C. Birch is Dean and Miller Professor of Biblical Theology at Wesley Theological Seminary. He is an ordained United Methodist minister in the Baltimore-Washington Annual Conference. He is the author of numerous books and articles on the Old Testament, stewardship, and ethics.

Charles R. (Chuck) Foster is an ordained United Methodist minister and professor of Christian education who has written curriculum resources for youth and adults and several books for leaders in the church's education. He leads workshops on teaching and learning in the church and lectures in academic and congregational settings on the future of Christian education. He lives in Oregon and is married, has two children and one grandchild.

Alan Geyer, since his student days at Ohio Wesleyan and Boston Universities, has lived a double life in the fields of both theology and political science. In 2000, he was named Canon Ethicist at Washington National Cathedral. He is also Senior Scholar at the Churches' Center for Theology and Public Policy and was Professor of Political Ethics and Ecumenics at Wesley Theological Seminary from 1977 to 1996. An ordained United Methodist minister, he served pastorates in Cambridge, Massachusetts and Newark, New Jersey. He was research coordinator and principal writer for the United Methodist Bishops' 1986 Pastoral Letter and Foundation Document, *In Defense of Creation: The Nuclear Crisis and a Just Peace.* He is married to the co-author of these sessions, Barbara G. Green.

Barbara G. Green is Executive Director of the Churches' Center for Theology and Public Policy, an ecumenical center in Washington, DC specializing in studying public policy issues from the perspective of Christian faith. Before coming to the Churches' Center in 1998, for fifteen years she served as a policy advocate in the Washington Office of the Presbyterian Church (USA).There she specialized in international relations and military policy. She is translator of the forthcoming edition of Dietrich Bonhoeffer's *Discipleship* and co-author of *Lines in the Sand: Justice and the Gulf War.* She

is a clergywoman of the Presbyterian Church (USA) and a graduate of Yale University Divinity School. She is married to the co-author of these sessions, Alan Geyer.

Rebecca Laird lives in Madison, New Jersey with her family. For nearly two decades she has edited and written books and curriculum on the spiritual life. Rebecca began to learn the hard lessons of hospitality and community while working in a small urban church in San Francisco. One December day she visited a homeless church friend who had spent the previous week sleeping in the park and was now in the hospital suffering from hypothermia. Seeing this gentle man nearly lose his feet because the shelters were full, she first understood that hospitality isn't a luxury but a spiritual discipline for the community of faith.

Mary Elizabeth Mullino Moore is Professor of Religion and Education and Director of the Program for Women in Theology and Ministry at Candler School of Theology, Emory University, Atlanta, Georgia. She loves the textures of God's earth and the beauty of God's diverse people. One of her recent books is *Ministering with the Earth,* and she feels constantly challenged to live fully and courageously in this world where suffering abides alongside wonder. She and Allen have five children and seven grandchildren, adding much fun, complexity, and awe to daily life.

Sondra Ely Wheeler teaches Christian Ethics at Wesley Theological Seminary in Washington D.C. Her interest in stewardship arises from her work in biblical ethics and the Wesleyan tradition. In addition, she works in bioethics, the virtue tradition, and the history of moral theology.

V. Sue Zabel is Associate Professor and Director of the Practice in Ministry and Mission at Wesley Theological Seminary in Washington, D.C. She is also a field consultant with the Alban Institute, Bethesda, Maryland, and works with congregations and church-related organizations from many denominations. Her current research, writing, and consulting focus on identification and employment of individual and congregational spiritual gifts.

VIDEO PARTICIPANTS

Meryll Rose, host of the *Steward* videos, has been working in television for twenty years as a news reporter and anchor, host of the syndicated series "PM Magazine," producer of entertainment programming including the country music series "Crook & Chase," and for the last five years as the host of Nashville's top-rated daily magazine show, "Talk of the Town." Meryll has been a member of Brentwood United Methodist Church, Brentwood, Tennessee, for twenty-one years. She is a soloist with the Chancel Choir, teaches Sunday school in the Youth Department, and serves on the Staff-Parish Relations Committee. She is married to Dan Elkins and they have a daughter Lauren who is 18, a son Kevin who is 11, and a golden retriever Samson who is 3.

Sessions 1 and 12:

M. Garlinda Burton is editor of *Interpreter* magazine published nationally for United Methodist laity and clergy and is an active member of Hobson United Methodist Church, a rejuvenating, multiracial, inner-city church in Nashville, Tennessee. "I believe that every good gift from God is given to us to pass it on and to be used to better the lives of God's people. Giving the best of yourself is sometimes a chore, but it is always a blessing."

Frank Trotter has been the senior pastor at the Reisterstown United Methodist Church in the Baltimore-Washington Annual Conference since July 1, 1984. He is currently working on a degree in clinical psychology at Loyola University in Baltimore, Maryland. Frank believes that stewardship—the care of all of God's creation—is one of the most important challenges facing Christians as we move into the twenty-first century. Holistic stewardship tells us that everything is connected—personal blessings, national blessings, global blessings—and that we are called to take our place at God's side as partners in creation.

Sessions 2 and 3:

John Pitney is an ordained minister in The United Methodist Church. He drives his electric car to visit elders of First United Methodist Church in Eugene, Oregon. As adjunct staff of the Western Small Church/Rural Life Center, he helps bring faith into discussions of food system globalization, sustainable agriculture, and worker justice. A member of Oregon Interfaith Network for Earth Concerns, he is available, on invitation, to lead worship and workshops on stewardship matters ranging from faith and global warming to how to be the church in a society of affluence. John has two albums of his own songs recorded to help us discuss these things in faith.

Joyce Johnson Rouse is a singer, songwriter, actor, activist, and entertainer from Brentwood, Tennessee, who performs as Earth Mama. From school assemblies to international conferences, she empowers audiences to positive action. Joyce employs her expertise in environmental science, humor, and motivation through music to reach audiences with practical ideas for making the planet a safer, more beautiful place.

Sessions 4 and 5:

David Radford Thomas was reared in a United Methodist parsonage in Kentucky. David graduated from Vanderbilt University and worked as a securities analyst. He then earned his master's degree in theology from the University of Bristol, England, writing his dissertation on the life and ministry of John Wesley. After working in corporate finance with Bakers Trust Company, he attended the Candler School of Theology, Emory University, Atlanta. David married Karen Elaine Muselman in September, 1995. They have one son, Luke, who was 3 weeks old at the time of the videotaping. Currently David serves as senior pastor of Centenary United Methodist Church, Lexington, Kentucky. Piano, violin, and dulcimer, along with hiking, tennis, and travel, are among his avocational interests.

Eugene Kim is currently the pastor of Cornerstone English Ministry, which is a quickly growing Asian-America Generation X church in Englewood, New Jersey. A graduate of Wesley Theological Seminary, Eugene has been a youth pastor, campus minister, and a pastor of a Caucasian church. He has a passion and a special calling to reach unchurched young adults regardless of race and cultural background.

Sessions 6 and 7:

Karla M. Kincannon, a United Methodist clergywoman, artist, and certified Healing Touch practitioner, has been a spiritual director for over fifteen years. Currently on the faculty at Stillpoint, a school for spiritual direction and contemplative prayer located in Nashville, she has taught the basic spiritual practices of the Christian faith and helped individuals unlock the mysteries of the inner life by using the creative process. She believes the power, motivation, and courage to be a good steward of God's creation comes from rooting oneself in God through the use of the spiritual disciplines.

Trace Haythorn serves as the associate pastor for adult education at Westminster Presbyterian Church in Nashville, Tennessee. He is committed to helping congregations explore the corporate and personal dimensions of stewardship, focusing particularly on the ways we welcome and include the gifts of all people in faith communities. He lives in Nashville with his wife Mary and their two young children, Jacob and Martha.

Sessions 8 and 9:

Robert (Bob) B. Coleman is in his fifth year as pastor of Edgehill United Methodist Church in Nashville, Tennessee. Edgehill UMC is an active, diverse congregation committed to justice ministries in a low-income neighborhood of south Nashville. As an adjunct professor, Bob also teaches two courses, "The Church and the Poor" and "The Church in Urban Contexts" at Vanderbilt Divinity School. Prior to coming to Edgehill, Bob has served as pastor to small rural churches, as a campus minister, and as an associate minister in a large multi-staffed urban church.

Myron McCoy is the senior pastor of St. Mark United Methodist Church, currently the largest African American United Methodist congregation in metropolitan Chicago. Married and the father of three sons, Myron is also actively involved in serving with a number of groups and organizations across the church and community as a steward. He says, "Christian stewardship for me is concerned about all of life. It is about who we are, whose we are, and how we are to live. Stewardship is about our holding in trust, being totally accountable and responsible for something or someone before God."

Sessions 10 and 11:

Rusty Lawrence has been the Executive Director of Urban Housing Solutions for the last nine years. His work experiences include a range of nonprofit agencies and social issues both in the US and Latin America. His motivation for pursuing charitable endeavors comes from a combination of the role models of his parents and his belief that social causes make a difference.

Elise Moss is an associate pastor at Trinity United Methodist Church in Huntsville, Alabama. The main focus of her ministry is in the area of missions and stewardship. Prior to entering the ministry, she practiced law for over twenty years, mostly with Legal Services agencies, where she handled a wide variety of civil cases, including public interest class actions.

Storytellers:

Ray Buckley, Sessions 4, 5, and 8, is Director of Native American Communications for United Methodist Communications in Nashville, Tennessee. He is of Tlingit, Lakota, and Scottish descent and he spent the early part of his life on

the Pine Ridge Indian Reservation in South Dakota. Ray is the author and illustrator of two books, *God's Love is Like . . .* and *The Give-Away: A Christmas Story*, both published by Abingdon Press. *The Give-Away* was featured on the CBS Christmas Eve special produced by the National Council of Churches. Ray has taught in Nigeria and Ghana and, in addition to his duties at UMCom, he serves as lecturer in Native American Studies at two universities in the Nashville area. In 1996 Ray received the Amy Crotts award for humanitarianism from the State of Tennessee.

Adora Dupree, Sessions 7, 10, 11, and 12, has been a professional storyteller since 1984. During that time, she has developed her own work for performance and residency. Adora has also taught at the Southeast Institute for Education in the Theater at the University of Tennessee, Chattanooga. She has performed at and been an on-site artist for the Tennessee Arts Academy of the Tennessee Arts Commission. As Arts in Education Director for the Knoxville Arts Council, she directed the Knoxville Institute for the Arts and created the African American Appalachian Arts Exposition. Her performance work expands knowledge of

African and African American history and traditions, celebrates families and ordinary heroes, teaches the dangers of drug use, enfolds listeners in the art of storytelling, and inspires others to their own creative potential.

Dayton Edmonds, Session 2, is a Native American storyteller from Omark, Washington. He leads workshops, seminars, and lecture series using his storytelling ability. He consults with churches, libraries, and schools in the areas of cultural sensitivity and relationships to nature and the earth. Dayton has been active in setting up an arts fair for children in his area. He is retired from the General Board of Global Ministries of the United Methodist Church where he was a Church and Community Worker.

Michael Williams, Sessions 1, 6, and 9, is a writer, teacher, and storyteller who serves as pastor of Blakemore United Methodist Church in Nashville, Tennessee. He is General Editor of *The Storyteller's Companion to the Bible* series published by Abingdon Press. Michael is father to Sarah and Elizabeth and husband to Margaret.